RETURN OF THE WHITE BOOK

True Stories of God at Work in Southeast Asia

HIDDEN HEROES 4

RETURN OF THE WHITE BOOK

True Stories of God at Work in

Southeast Asia

REBECCA DAVIS

CF4•K

10 9 8 7 6 5 4
Copyright © 2014 Rebecca Davis
ISBN: 978-1-78191-292-8

Published in 2014 and reprinted in 2017,
2020 and 2021
by
Christian Focus Publications,
Geanies House, Fearn, Tain,
Ross-shire, IV20 1TW,
Great Britain

Cover design by Daniel van Straaten
Cover illustration by Fred Apps
Other illustrations by Jeff Anderson
Printed and bound by Nørhaven, Denmark

Unless otherwise stated the Scripture quotations are from
The Holy Bible, English Standard Version, copyright
© 2001 by Crossway Bibles, a division of
Good News Publishers.
Used by permission. All rights reserved.

To my brothers and sisters of the Karen tribes of Southeast Asia

To access more information and activities, see the *Return of the White Book* page at the Christian Focus website at www.christianfocus.com.

Contents

MAP OF BURMA AND SIAM

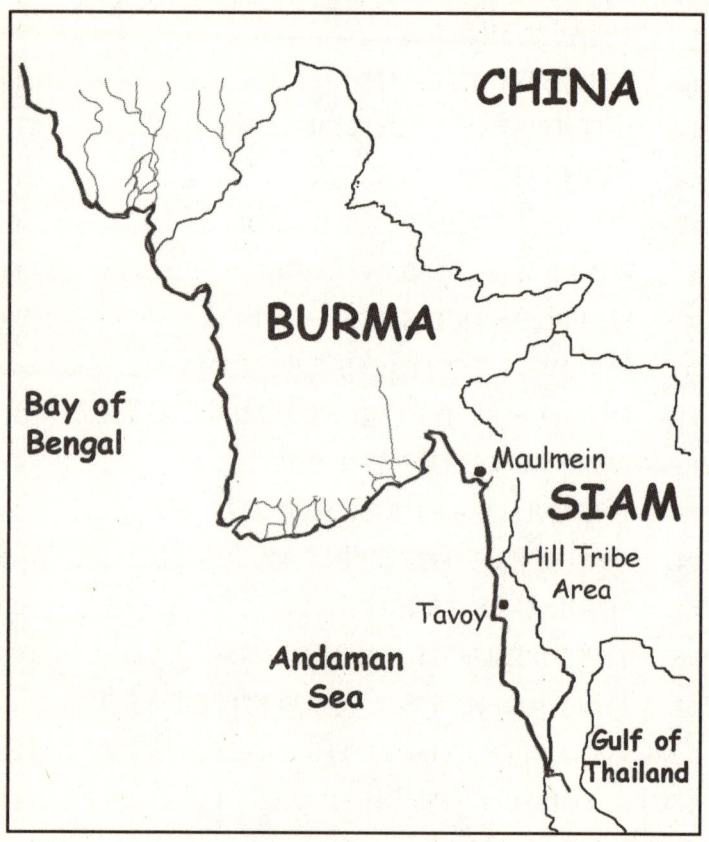

1. KEEPER OF THE STORIES

In the land of Burma, the Burmans ruled. With their education and their fine clothes and their grand books, they controlled the land.

All the tribes in the hill country lived in fear of the Burmans, fear of capture and slavery. One of the hill tribes, the Karens, kept moving from place to place as their only hope of safety.

Every place they moved, they carried their ancient stories with them. Stories of despair. Stories of hope.

One night, around a small campfire, an old man sat cross-legged, his eyes darting from one face to another. A teenage boy named Thabew hurried to sit next to his uncle. The dark-skinned people, young and old, long black hair flowing, jostled for position around the flames.

Parents, children, young people, all gazed at the old man in awe. He was the Keeper of the Stories, and the Stories must be passed on. His high, clear voice began.

After Yuwah made Thanai and Ew, He put them in a garden. It was more beautiful than any garden of our world. It was full of bananas, lychees, pomelos, durians, and pomegranates.

Then Yuwah said to them, "I have given you this beautiful garden. You will tend it. I will visit you here, and walk and talk with you. Pray to Me each day."

Yuwah said, "Seven kinds of fruit I have put in this garden. Eat freely of all of them. Except one. If you eat of that one," Yuwah said, "you will die."

Thanai and Ew had many children and many grandchildren. When Yuwah came to visit them and walk with them, all their children and grandchildren sang praises to Yuwah.

Then, Mukawli came.

Mukawli said to the man and woman, "Why are you here? What do you eat?"

Thanai and Ew said, "Our Father Yuwah put us here. We eat all the delicious fruit He has given us. We want for nothing."

But Mukawli wished to trap them. He said, "Let me see your fruit."

Thanai and Ew showed Mukawli everything. They described the color and texture and juiciness of the durian and the banana and the pomelo.

But then they came to the forbidden tree. They said, "We know not about this fruit, because our Father Yuwah has told us we must not eat it, or we will die."

Mukawli said, "O my children, your Father Yuwah does not love you. He doesn't want you to have the richest and sweetest fruit of all. He wants to keep it from you because then you will have powers like Him! You will be able to fly up to heaven or go down into the depths of the earth!"

Thanai and Ew received Mukawli's words with open ears. Then Mukawli said, "O my children, my heart is not like the heart of Yuwah. I love you and I want to see you prosper. I will always speak the truth to you. If you eat that fruit, you will prosper."

Thanai answered Mukawli and said, "I will not eat, because Yuwah has forbidden it," and he turned and walked away. But Ew stayed, to listen more. Mukawli spoke more fair words to her of the wonders of the life to come if Ew would but eat that magical fruit. "My daughter," he said, "I seek to persuade you because I love you."

Finally, Ew reached out her hand and took the fruit and ate it.

Mukawli could hardly contain his delight, and he trembled as he spoke his next words. He said, "Woman, you must give the fruit to your husband. Tell him of the wonders of its sweetness. Tell him of the wonders of its powers."

Not long after, Ew convinced Thanai to eat. Then the woman cried, "My husband has eaten the fruit, O Mukawli!"

Then Mukawli laughed and laughed and laughed. "I have conquered you! You listened to my voice and obeyed me, and now you are my slaves! You must obey me till the end!"

The next morning Yuwah came to visit, to walk, and to receive praises. But all was silent.

Yuwah said, "Thanai! Ew! You have eaten of the forbidden fruit!" The man and the woman came out

and hung their heads in shame before Yuwah. They had no words.

"You have disobeyed my commands," Yuwah said. "You will grow old. You will fall ill. You will die." Then Yuwah went away forever.

Soon one of the children of the man and woman became ill. Thanai and Ew knew they could not reach Yuwah, because He had departed from them forever. So they went to Mukawli, because now he was their master.

"What shall we do for our sick child, Mukawli?" they asked.

Mukawli threw back his head and laughed. "You are my slaves!" he cried out. "Now you must offer sacrifices to my servants, the nats. They are the ones who cause sicknesses, and accidents too. They will control the weather and the seasons and the wild animals and war and life and death and everything that happens to you. If you want peace in your lives, you must offer sacrifices to the nats. Now, if you want to know what to do for anything, anything in your life, you must learn to read the bones of the jungle fowl and the dung of the pig. To make war, to marry, to plant, to travel. Do nothing without finding out what the nats command. That is the only way to keep the nats from destroying you. That is the only way to peace."

The old man's last words lingered in the air.

Throughout the story, the listeners had been reacting with strong emotions. Fear at the mention of Mukawli. Anger at Ew's betrayal. Hopelessness at their enslavement to Mukawli.

But the old man's last words trembled before them like the shout of a mocking nat. Because there was never peace.

As young Thabew listened, he knew as well as the old man that nats could never be trusted any more than their master Mukawli. That's why his people had to learn all those magic words and rituals. That's why he, Thabew, tried to scare the nats away by wearing a tiger's tooth and a bear's claw.

A hatred rose up inside him. He hated those nats. He hated Mukawli. He hated this slavery. And then he ducked his head. His eyes darted here and there, fearful lest the nats discover his unformed thoughts.

The boy raised his eyes to the countless stars glittering in the blackness. That's where Yuwah had gone—somewhere beyond those stars.

"Yuwah is lost to us!" The old man cried out, raising his arms in despair.

"Not forever, grandfather," a younger man answered respectfully. "The pale brother will come."

"Yes, someday." The old man nodded, clinging to their only hope. "The pale brother will come to the

Karen nation, with the white book. He will show us the way back to Yuwah. Someday."

The small circle of listeners gazed into the dying embers. They despaired.

They hoped.

See Thinking Further for Chapter 1 on page 136.

2. WAITING FOR THE PALE BROTHER

The rice paddy fields had sprouted. The men had dreamed their dreams and offered sacrifices and read the bird bones in order to find just the right place to cut down the trees and plant their rice. And now those ridges on the hills showed shoots of bright green.

At the first light of day, Thabew and the other men climbed down the ladder from the village sleeping house, to go out to the fields. There they would make more sacrifices and sing more chants, in hopes of persuading the nats to leave their paddy fields alone and let them harvest their rice.

The women and children climbed down too. The little boys were sent to catch some of the jungle fowl by the neck and give them to the men for the sacrifices.

While the men took the birds and made their way out to the field, the boys ran off to check their rat traps. While some of the women and girls trekked down to the river for the day's supply of water, others of them took their spinning and weaving tools outside and began to work on one of their many jobs— making clothes. While they worked, they sang. They sang in a low, mournful tone, in a minor key. It was an ancient song.

> *Long ago, Yuwah loved the Karen nation above all others,*
> *But because of their sins, He cursed them,*
> *And now they have no books.*
> *But He will again have mercy on them, and love them above all others.*

A boy came running with excitement, holding a rat by the tail. He popped it into a basket and began to prepare a fire to cook it for his family's breakfast.

The men built an altar at the paddy field and offered a jungle fowl. They said, "Let this please you, O master nat of the hills, O master nat of the land, master nat of fire, master nat of heat and cold. We want to make you comfortable. Therefore, moderate the heat of the soil and let the paddy be good. Let the rice be good."

In the village some women and girls took the cotton that had been carded and smoothed out. They put it on their spinning wheels and began to spin it into thread. While they spun, they sang. Long and low, sad and wailing.

The Karen was the older brother, and received all the words of Yuwah.
But Yuwah departed with our younger brother, the pale foreigner.
He went with Yuwah away to the West.
Yuwah gave him power to cross waters and reach lands,
Then Yuwah went up to heaven.

Other boys came with the animals they had caught in their pit traps and small bamboo box traps, rabbits, squirrels, crows, and more rats. Always rats. With excitement they slit the throats and prepared to cook them.

Thabew and the other men built the second altar and slit the throat of another jungle fowl, smearing the blood around the altar. "We have prepared this for you," they muttered to the nats. "We are doing you good. We want to make you comfortable. We want to be unafraid of the bad omens."

Some women took the cotton that had already been spun and lowered it carefully into a pot of steaming indigo, coloring some of it light blue, some medium blue, some midnight blue. They dipped some into pots of boiling stick-lac, to dye it brick red. The young girls, their simple smocks hanging to their knees, watched and learned. And they sang.

When Yuwah had departed,
The Karens became slaves to the Burmans,
The Burmans made them work bitterly,
Till many dropped down dead in the jungle.

In the midst of their sufferings,
The Karens remembered the ancient sayings of the elders,
That Yuwah would still save them,
That a Karen king would yet appear.
When he arrives, everything will be happy,
And even lions and leopards will lose their savageness.

So in their deep afflictions the Karen people prayed.
We can endure these sufferings no longer. Alas! Where is Yuwah?

The men muttered their dark prayers, their nat chants, till dark. They killed one jungle fowl after another, burning the feathers and smearing the blood. "O Guardian Bird of the field, do not let anything eat the paddy in the plot where you watch," they muttered. But they knew that even though they prayed to the spirits, still they and their families would have to stay up all night every night till rice harvest, to drive away the deer and wild pigs, the rats and birds that would seek to eat their rice paddies, or the wild elephants that could trample the entire field.

The boys got their blowguns and traps ready, to prepare for guarding the fields.

The women and girls would have to take their turns in the fields too. But they would also soon undertake the weaving of the coarse cloth that made the colorful skirts they wore under their smocks. And they would sing. The men and boys would join them in the song, though no one was quite sure what the songs meant.

Our ancestors said that when our younger brothers come back,
The pale foreigners who were able to keep company with Yuwah,
The Karens will be happy.

Our ancestors told us, "Children and grandchildren,
It will not come in our days, But it will come in yours.
If it comes by land, then weep. If it comes by water, then laugh."
This is why the Karens long for those who will come by water.

It was a song of great sadness, but a song of hope. Thabew clenched his fists, as he did all the time now. Would the pale brother one day come by water?

But when the first Christian missionary came from America to Burma—by water—that missionary, Adoniram Judson, had no idea that these hill tribes even existed.

See Thinking Further for Chapter 2 on page 136.

3. A FIRE INSIDE ME

One day years later, Adoniram Judson leaned forward in his chair and rested his elbows on his knees, speaking to a younger missionary who had been in Burma only a few months. "I know this is difficult, brother," he said. "But you know that we need to open a new mission station at Tavoy. And surely the Lord is making it clear to you that you're the right man to do it."

The missionary he spoke to was George Boardman. During his short time in Burma, George had been responsible for building this flourishing mission station at Maulmein.

Adoniram Judson had waited seven years to see the first Burmese man come to Christ. But now, almost every week hungry seekers from among the Burmese people were coming. George and his wife Sarah stayed busy telling others the good news of Jesus Christ and teaching in the school.

Tavoy? It was almost two hundred miles down the coast, with only a British military base there now. Mission work would start from scratch.

The younger missionary looked up with a smile. "The Lord will be our helper," he said. "Sarah and I will go forward."

"One more thing," Adoniram said. "You know that man Thabew, the one from that wild Karen tribe, wants to go with you.

"Yes," answered George. "You said he was almost ready for baptism. Haven't I seen him trying to learn to read the Burmese Bible?"

"Yes, a little, and the light of Christ does seem to be piercing his heart. But don't expect too much of

him, because he's a Karen, and the Karens don't learn as quickly as the Burmans. And be careful of his violent temper—that's the reason he still hasn't been baptized, you know."

On March 29, 1828, the Boardmans stood on the boat to go down the coast, waving goodbye to the Judsons and other missionaries, on their way to Tavoy.

Near George Boardman stood another man, a man he didn't know well. It was Thabew, gazing out at the sunlight sparkling on the Bay of Bengal. Even though Thabew wore the robe of the Burmans, his long, loose black hair still gave him a wild look.

"Ko Thabew," the young missionary said respectfully, "tell me how you came to Mr. Judson. Did you really murder people?"

"Huh," Thabew grunted. "More than thirty. My rage was great." He hung his head. "The Burmans came and took some of my people slaves—they took all our rice and all that we had, and they carried away our women." His voice shook, and he gripped his fists. "Almost no one was left of my tribe. I killed some of the Burmans, but they took me captive and made me a slave."

"All the Karens live in fear of the Burmans, don't they?" George Boardman asked gently.

"Fear, all the time," answered Thabew. "That's why we try to hide away in the hills. The Burmans don't care if my people starve. And they do starve. I have hated the Burmans. But Teacher Judson showed kindness to me. He paid my slave debt and set me free. He told me about Jesu Cree, and I have believed."

George Boardman gazed at this mysterious man who seemed so different from the Burmans. "Tell me about the worship of your people," he said.

"Worship?"

"Yes, you know. Who do they bow down to? What do they honor?"

"My people bow down to none. We honor none."

"Do you mean to say that your people have no images like these Burmans?" Even now, as the ship sailed, George could point to images here and there set up along the coast, images of Buddha, images of other gods.

"No, no images." Thabew spoke with certainty.

"No religion, then. Interesting."

Thabew was quiet.

"Ko Thabew, you have said you want to be baptized. Tell me why."

Thabew hesitated, searching for words in the Burmese language. "I know that Jesu Cree is the true one," he said. "The one from Sky Father. Ko Judson told me this. I read it in the white book."

"And are you aware of your own sin, your badness?"

This time Thabew didn't hesitate. "Oh, yes!" he said. "I was a very bad man."

"And what did Jesus do for you?" the pale missionary pressed gently.

"He died. He showed great love. He took me from my sin." Thabew turned earnest eyes toward George Boardman. "I still fight with anger. There is a fire inside me."

"I pray that Jesus Christ will turn that fire to a passion for Him." George opened a little book he held in his hand. It was a catechism written in the Burmese language, translated by Adoniram Judson's wife, Ann.

" 'Who is God?' " he read. He was about to read the answer when Thabew lifted his eyes to the sky and said, "He is a Being without beginning or end, who is not subject to old age or death, but always is."

"So you have memorized this catechism, Thabew?"

"Some of it, Teacher Boardman. It is in Burmese, and my eyes still grasp that language slowly."

"Yes." George nodded. He read the next question. " 'Who is Jesus?' "

Again Thabew lifted his eyes to heaven. "He is the Son of God, who, with compassion for His creatures, came into this world and suffered death in their place."

Thabew's eyes filled with tears and he gripped his fist. "My people need to hear this," he said. "There is a fire inside me."

See Thinking Further for Chapter 3 on page 136.

4. WHY HAVE YOU COME?

The news of George Boardman's arrival in Tavoy traveled quickly from person to person, from village to village. Finally it reached a village so far from Tavoy that it was almost across the border in Siam. The village was called Chikku.

"A pale teacher has come by water from Maulmein with a Karen man."

"Why has he come?" asked one named Moung Kya.

"To preach the words of Yuwah, who made heaven and earth."

"We must go and see."

On the morning of May 1st, 1828, George Boardman looked up from his work. Thabew stood there. "Teacher Boardman," he said, "some of my people have come to see you."

Quickly the pale missionary went outside to see a crowd of Karen men, about thirty of them. They had long black hair like Thabew, but it was knotted on their heads and held with strange combs made of bamboo. Instead of the Burmese robe that Thabew wore, they wore dirty cotton smocks that fell from their shoulders to their knees.

"I am Moung Kya," said one with a large, sharp animal tooth hanging down from his ear. "We have come to ask you who you are and what you bring us." He spoke Burmese, but with such a heavy Karen accent that George had trouble understanding him.

"I bring you a message of good news from the true Sky Father." The missionary tried to speak in simple words, knowing that the Burmese language was difficult for them.

Moung Kya translated, and the men all looked back and forth at each other. Sky Father? Who was that?

"Where do you come from?" asked the missionary.

"We walked three days to come here," replied the man. "We live in the mountains."

Thabew listened and added, "My people are scattered all over the mountains, in small villages. The Burmans persecute us always. We must run from place to place."

Maybe that's why they have such a wild look, thought the missionary. "Who do you worship?" George Boardman asked the same question he had asked of Thabew. "Do you honor any image or ancestor? Do you hold high the name of any god?"

The men looked back and forth at each other again. No one spoke.

Atheists, all of them, the young missionary thought.

"I am a Buddhist," said one young man. "I honor the Buddha."

Several men spoke quickly in their native tongue. Thabew explained. "That man traded with the Burmans and took their religion. It is not our Karen way."

For a moment there was silence as the visitors looked at Thabew. *Who are these people?* thought George. *I've been occupied just trying to understand the Burmese culture, and here is a completely new one. They don't have any understanding of any god.* He eyed their scant, dirty rags, so different from the bright clean colors of the Burmans. "Ko Thabew, if you'll translate for me, I'll try to begin to explain," he said.

The new Christian nodded. George Boardman began thinking about what he wanted to say, but before he could speak, another man stood forward, wearing a similar animal tooth over his ear and dozens of necklaces over his smock that looked to be made of teeth and seeds and stones and other small things. He spoke in the Karen language. Thabew translated.

"Respected Teacher." The man bowed. "I am Moung So, the chief of the village of Chikku. We come with a request. More than ten years ago, a pale brother came to us. He told us that there was one living and true Sky Father, as you said. He gave us many rules to follow. He told us to give up eating pig meat or jungle fowl. He told us ceremonies that we must keep, to be pleasing to the Sky Father.

"Respected Teacher, that pale brother gave us a book. All of us knew about books, but none in our village had ever had one before. None can tell what is written in the book. The Guardian of the Book instructs us how to honor the book and follow the ceremonies."

So they do have a religion, mused the young missionary. *It is Book Worship.*

"The Burmans mock us and persecute us for our book. But now that the pale foreigners are here, the Burmans are afraid to persecute us. This means that we can come to Tavoy to inquire of you. We want the Guardian of the Book to bring his book to you to show you."

"I'll be glad to see it."

"The Guardian of the Book will come to you. But I ask also that after the season of rain, when the sky is dry, that you come to our village and explain your teachings. If you cannot come, we ask that you send one of your men. We must know."

"Thank you," answered George. "I hope I can come soon, after the business here is less pressing. Here, this is a little booklet I can give you. It tells about the true religion, about Sky Father and His Son Jesus Christ. I do apologize that it's in Burmese." He handed them a booklet written by Adoniram Judson, *A Creed, in Twelve Articles; or, A Summary of the Doctrine of the Lord Jesus Christ. for the People of Burma.*

The men listened as Thabew tried to explain in their language. But mainly, they wanted to hold that book— its pages were very white.

Moung Kya reached out his hand for it, trembling. He said, "A young man in our village can read this. He will read it to us."

They bowed low and departed, talking among themselves in excitement.

George Boardman watched them walk away, far away back to the mountains. *Strange*, he thought. *It was years before the Burmans would listen. Why are atheists so interested in learning the truth of God?*

See Thinking Further for Chapter 4 on page 137.

5. IS IT THE LOST BOOK OF YUWAH?

The people of Chikku said to each other, "Look! Look at this book!" They took turns holding the small booklet with the very white pages.

"Is it a book of the Karens?"

"No, it's written in the language of the Burmans. But listen! Listen to these words!" The young man who knew the Burmese language read to them. " 'There is one only eternal God, who is excellent beyond understanding. He is almighty, all-knowing, the Maker of all things.' "

"This is Yuwah!" said someone. "This speaks the same as our own words of our great Yuwah in our ancient traditions! *'Yuwah is eternal, his life is long. Yuwah is immortal, his life is long. One age he dies not. Two ages he dies not. He is perfect in excellent qualities. Age upon age, he dies not. All things in heaven and on earth, O children and grandchildren, Yuwah created them.'* "

"These words in this book are good words! These are true words!" News of the small white book traveled from village to village to village.

* * *

Less than two weeks after the mysterious visitors from Chikku had departed, George Boardman found some of them again at his door. He recognized Moung So, the chief. And there was Moung Kya, the man who had first spoken to him. The third man was young, maybe only twenty years old.

"We bring you gifts, Respected Teacher," said Moung Kya in his halting Burmese. He held out a crude basket of bamboo, filled with large duck eggs.

"Please," said George. "Speak your own language. One of my men will translate."

Thabew came down the ladder from the house to help.

"The Karen teacher, Apya Thi, is the Guardian of the Book," said Moung So, the chief. "He is very sick and could not come with us today, which gives him great sorrow. He'll come at the end of the season of rain, to bring the Great Book for you to examine. We want you to tell us if it is a book of your God."

"Did you find anyone to read the little booklet I gave your people last time?" the young missionary asked.

The youngest man stepped forward and spoke in Burmese that George Boardman could understand. "Respected Teacher, I am Sekyi. I can read Burmese, Respected Teacher. I translated your small book to my father, the Guardian of the Book. When he heard those words, he began to weep. He believed every word. For the last many days my father and I have gone from house to house, and my father commands people to listen to me read the book. He says that the lost book of our fathers has returned to us. Everywhere, my people believe. If you would come to our people, or if one of your helpers would come, many more would believe these good words."

"But what is it you're believing?" George asked, incredulous. "Do you believe there is but one God?"

"Yes. We have never worshiped the many gods of the Burmans. Our ancient teachers have told us, 'O children and grandchildren! Do not worship idols. If you worship them you obtain no advantage thereby, while you increase your sins exceedingly.' "

"I thought you were atheists. I thought you didn't worship anyone."

"The God of our people has been separated from us, and we knew not how to worship him. But your small book tells us truth." Sekyi opened the booklet and read, " 'According to the Scriptures, man, at the beginning, was made upright and holy.' This we believe, Respected Teacher." He continued to read. " 'But listening to the devil'—we know that this is Mukawli—'man went against the commands of God.

Then he fell away from his good place. He became full of sin and deserving of God's punishment.' " All this we believe and know to be true. But we have many questions, many questions."

"Well, what are some of your questions?"

"You say, 'According to the Scriptures.' We know not these Scriptures."

"They are the Word of God. The Bible." He picked up his English Bible. "Mr. Judson is translating it into the Burmese language."

"We need that book in our own Karen language. But our written language is lost. Will the pale brother help us regain it?"

"We need more workers," said the missionary. "But I hope we can."

The men looked at each other again, as if they were trying to figure out which question was the most important. "If we turn through Jesu Cree, how will we appease the nats? They'll be very angry."

"Nats? What are nats?"

"The spirits of the trees and the rocks and the jungle fowl and the wild pigs and tigers and other animals. The spirits of the rain and the wind and sickness. The servants of Mukawli."

"Evil spirits? Did your Guardian of the Great Book teach you that?"

The men stared at the missionary. They looked back and forth at each other as if unable to comprehend. "We have always known this to be true," one said.

"Yes, we have much work to do," George Boardman murmured. "You cannot practice spirit appeasement and at the same time worship the Great Jehovah through Jesus Christ."

"Our teachings are the same as yours, Respected Teacher," Moung Kya said politely. "We want to spend three days with you and learn from you before we return to our village."

"Respected Teacher." Sekyi came forward again. "My father, the Guardian of the Great Book, has asked that I stay with the Foreign Teacher for two or three years. I know a little Burmese, but this way I can learn more, and I will be able to more clearly explain the way of God to my people."

Extraordinary. George thought. *Absolutely extraordinary.*

Three mornings later, these same Karen men went early to the river with the pale missionary and Thabew. It was finally time for the promised baptism of Thabew, the first Karen Christian.

"I baptize you, my brother …"

Brother? The pale man called the Karen man brother!

"… in the Name of the Father and of the Son and of the Holy Spirit. You are buried with Him in the likeness of His death." George Boardman lowered Thabew into the water. "You are raised with Him in the likeness of His resurrection." Thabew reappeared, dripping wet.

"We have much to learn about the truth of this way," said Moung So. "This ceremony is a mystery."

"We're determined that we will worship as you teach us," the Moung Kya, "whatever the cost! Respected Teacher?"

"Yes?" George was climbing out of the river onto the bank, shivering.

"If you cannot go with us now, we request that you send with us this Karen man, this worshiper of the true Yuwah, to explain this way more clearly to us. We have listened to him for three days, and we understand his words better than yours."

George Boardman smiled. "Do you want to go, Ko Thabew?"

"Yes!" Thabew lifted his hands to heaven. "I want to go to my people! The passion of Jesu Cree burns a fire in my bones! I want to show my people the true Way of the true God Yuwah!"

"Do you know enough, do you understand enough about the true God, to teach your people?"

"I know little and understand little, Teacher Boardman. But I know and understand that Jesu Cree is the way to Yuwah. I know that none of my people's customs and works will help us reach God. Faith alone is the way. I know the power of Jesu Cree over sin. I can read a little of the Burmese books. I can answer a few of the questions."

"Well, then, go with God. Go with Yuwah, as you call Him."

Thabew changed into a simple Karen smock. As he was saying goodbye to his wife for a journey into the hills, Moung Kya spoke again to Teacher Boardman. "The Guardian of the Book will come, after the season of rain," he assured him. "We will do what you say. If you say that our Book is a bad book, we'll burn it. After the season of rain, we'll build you a zayat in our village. Then we'll call the Karens from all over the mountains to listen to you."

George watched the two other visitors depart, with Thabew beside them. *May God go with you, my brother,* the missionary prayed. *Only just baptized, and already a missionary to his people. Lord, do a great work among these sons of the wilderness.*

See Thinking Further for Chapter 5 on page 137

6. MORE! MORE!

As Thabew traveled and spoke, people listened. "You come from the pale brother? You have a book? What does it say? Who is this Jesu Cree? We didn't know about him! We knew only Mukawli and the nats!" They listened. They wondered.

And some of them believed.

Only four days after Thabew had left him, George Boardman looked out his window, watching the pounding rain. He knew that beyond his view the creeks and rivers would be swollen beyond passing.

So it didn't surprise him when he saw Thabew returning to the mission house, holding a large palm leaf over his head, which was still flowing down with water.

"You weren't able to get to the village?" the missionary called.

"No, Teacher Boardman," Thabew gasped as he climbed the bamboo ladder and entered the door.

"Too much rain, and the streams are too swollen. I couldn't cross."

"Take heart, my brother. You can go to your people after the rainy season."

"But I did go to my people! I couldn't go to Chikku village with our visitors, but I found many who wanted to hear my good words. I brought two of them with me."

George looked outside in the rain and saw, sure enough, there were two new Karen men waiting to hear more of the good words from the pale brother, their black hair knotted and held with small bamboo combs. Both of them also held the large palm leaves over their heads, but they stood with their long cotton smocks dripping wet.

The two young men climbed the ladder into the hut. One of them bowed and said, "I am resolved to become a Christian. I am brother to a great chief. I believe these good words Ko Thabew speaks to us. But we ask that after the season of rain you come yourself, pale brother, and teach us from your great Book."

"I am Sau Quala," said the other, who looked to be in his upper teens. "Mine was the first house that Ko Thabew came to. I must hear more."

A few days later, two more men came. "We heard the true words about Yuwah from Ko Thabew," they said. "We want to believe what you teach us."

George took the little booklet and read, as Thabew translated. "God knew that mankind would fall in sin and be ruined. So in His mercy He chose some to save from sin and hell and give to His Son Jesus Christ." He began to explain these words. The men raised their eyebrows in agreement, but their eyes still showed some questions.

Then Thabew began to speak. He spoke in Karen so quickly that Teacher Boardman couldn't follow any of his words at all. But the eyes of the visiting men began to light up. Their faces showed what their hearts felt— this was the truth they had long waited for.

"Brother, truly these are the words of Yuwah," one man said. "Come to our village and tell us more."

Thabew began to make more expeditions, go farther, preach longer. Sekyi, the young Karen man who had come to live with Teacher Boardman, went with him as his guide. Together they did their best to explain the words from the small booklet Adoniram Judson had written.

"All the people in every village," Ko Thabew cried when he returned, "all of them listen to these words. All want to believe on Jesu Cree to show them the way to Yuwah!"

The next month six more new Karen men came. "We have traveled three days," they said. "Many people are believing in the words of the small white book. We haven't seen the small book or the men who read it, but we heard about it. We wanted to come to hear the words of Yuwah from your own mouth. We'll stay two days and then go back to our people."

Almost every week, new Karens showed up at George Boardman's mission house. They went back to their villages to build zayats, temporary houses, in anticipation of the pale teacher coming to teach them after the rainy season had ended.

When Thabew and Sekyi returned from one preaching trip in September, Thabew said, "Teacher Boardman. I did go all the way to Chikku, the village of the Guardian of the Book. Those people listened to my words. They're building a zayat where you can teach them when you come after the season of rain. Moung So and Moung Kya are asking for baptism like me."

"Teacher Boardman," Sekyi added. "You preach the words of God to me, and I understand a little. Ko Thabew preaches to me, and I understand perfectly."

One day Thabew brought a young man wearing the long, clean robe of a Buddhist monk. Surely his dark skin and flat nose and wide-set eyes showed that he was a Karen. "He was sitting in a corner of the Buddhist pagoda."

The young man bowed and spoke in clear Burmese. "I was seeking the true religion. I didn't find it in the practices of my people. I turned from spirit fear, because there is no hope in that. I saw that the Burmans had a different religion, and their Buddhism gave me hope of reward for my good works. I've been fasting for two days, hoping for reward in the next life. But this man came to me." Here he looked at Thabew. "He told me that fasting will earn me no reward, and that there is a greater religion that is free. My heart longed to hear this religion." The young man stayed and listened, then departed with a booklet. The Christians prayed for him.

After about a month he returned, with three family members. "We want to learn more, Teacher Boardman," he said. Until late at night, then again very early in the morning, the voices in Thabew's room rose and fell. Questions and answers. Teaching and listening.

"This is the truth, the truth long promised to our ancestors," they kept saying.

The next afternoon the young man said, "Teacher Boardman, I want to learn from you, all the great teachings of your Holy Book. Many of my people will come, and I'll go to them. I want to live no longer in those heaps of bricks in the pagoda. I want to know and serve the eternal and true Father God."

"Teacher Boardman," Thabew said earnestly. "I wish you would write to America for more teachers to be sent out to help us."

Thabew was the first Karen missionary to his own people. He traveled so far, worked so hard, spoke so boldly, gave so willingly, that he became known as the Karen Apostle. The goal and passion of his life was to forsake everything to take the gospel of Jesus Christ to the Karen people.

See Thinking Further for Chapter 6 on page 138.

7. THE GUARDIAN OF THE BOOK

The Guardian of the Book cried out, "Come, all people! Come and worship! If you neglect worship, then when happiness comes, you will not be able to receive it!" Apya Thi had donned his great long robe and held out his rod. It was time to worship the Book.

There was the basket, with the Book inside, wrapped in rags. Apya Thi picked up the basket and held it high.

Around him, his young disciples banged the drums and clanged the gongs. Young and old, great and small, men and women, swarmed out of their huts toward him from every direction, even from distant villages, all who heard the drums and the gongs. No one wanted to miss happiness when it finally came.

"Bow, bow before me!" cried the Guardian of the Book. They bowed.

Then the parade began. Young Karen men went before him, brandishing their arrows and spears.

The drum-beaters and cymbal-clangers went behind, making a great noise.

And in this way they made their way to the zayat, the building where the people gathered to worship the Book—and the man who carried it. Women on one side, men on the other, they offered white cloth and pieces of silver to Apya Thi. But the Guardian of the Book took the silver to the stream, where he threw it in. "Burmese silver will end!" he cried. "Burmese worship will end! Sing and pray to Yuwah!" And the people sang as Apya Thi had taught them.

"This worship is excellent worship, the worship that Yuwah appointed;
Go up and worship on the mountain; the mountain that is the
seat of Yuwah.
He has come, he has come, Yuwah has come! Bring offerings of
early rice!
The golden ship has arrived, has arrived, it has arrived with
our younger brother!
The worship that Yuwah appointed, the great worship,
has reached the Karen people!
Oh! Think about the great worship! We will be unable to sleep."

Only about three months had passed since the first visit of the men of Chikku village to George Boardman's house in Tavoy. Now they stood outside his house once again, more excited than ever.

"The Guardian of the Book has come, Teacher!" Sekyi called. "The Karen men want you to see the Book."

After George had finished drinking his tea, he invited the men inside. Sarah, his wife, came with their little daughter to watch too. Some Burmese servants gathered as well.

Apya Thi, the Guardian of the Book, flourished his long white robe, unlike any that George had seen. He held out his rod.

Then he bowed low and spoke, while Sekyi translated. "Respected Teacher, I am Apya Thi. We, your humble servants, have come from the jungle to lay before you a book, and to ask you if it is good or bad, true or false. We know nothing of God or his ways. For twelve years we have bowed before this book, as we were told to do. But we are ignorant, we have no written language, so we cannot read this book.

"Now, from the small white book you gave us we have heard about the Good News of Jesu Cree," the Guardian of the Book continued. "We know what you teach is Truth, and we wish to know if this book contains the teachings of that Good News. We know that you can settle the question and teach us the true way of happiness."

What was the book?

Everyone watched, wide-eyed, as the old man produced a large bamboo basket. Inside the basket lay heaps upon heaps of rags. Carefully, with the greatest tenderness, Apya Thi began to unfold these rags.

Reaching in, the old man pulled out an old, tattered book. The writing on the cover and spine were too worn to read.

The young missionary took the book gently. He opened it to see pages and pages of charts. Then, as he turned a page, his eyes fell on these words: *The grace of our Lord Jesus Christ, and the love of God, and the fellowship of the Holy Ghost, be with us all evermore. Amen.*

Then he flipped back to the front. *The Book of Common Prayer*, it said. With the Psalms. Published in England.

All the Karen men around him watched as he gently turned the pages. It seemed that they were barely breathing, waiting for the word from the Respected Teacher.

"It is a good book," Teacher Boardman said finally. When Sekyi translated, the men breathed a sigh of relief, all together.

"But it is not good to worship it," he added. The men's eyes filled with grief.

"You should worship only the true God. This book tells about Him."

The men stayed for hours. For hour after hour George Boardman explained the truths in the little booklet, the one that Adoniram Judson had written in Burmese. Thabew translated.

"Is it true then," Apya Thi finally asked, "that I have no merit from worshiping this book? Does this not give me any goodness before Yuwah?"

"No," George answered. "All your goodness must come through Jesus Christ."

The old man's shoulders sagged. He sighed finally and said, "It is good."

When the Karens prepared to leave, the old man took up his sorcerer robe again. "This was given to me many years ago," he said. He squared his shoulders and raised his head. For twelve years he had been the Guardian of the Book.

"But father," said Sekyi respectfully, "there is no good wearing such a robe. There is no goodness in that. It would be better to put it aside altogether."

Once again the old man looked down and let out a long, slow breath. "If Yuwah will not be pleased with this robe," he said, "then I'll send it drifting away on the stream out there. Here, take this." He handed Thabew his rod. "I have no need of this. I am no longer the authority."

As the Karen men walked back to the mountain wilderness home, the old man took his robe, tore it into pieces, and threw it into the stream. Some weeks later when he saw Thabew, he said, "No more will I practice book-worship and book-ceremonies. Now I will worship the eternal Yuwah and His great Son, Jesu Cree."

See Thinking Further for Chapter 7 on page 138.

8. FUNERAL BATTLE IN CHIKKU

A young man from the village of Chikku stood outside the door, breathing hard. "Teacher Boardman, I have run for three days to come to you. We wish for Ko Thabew and his wife."

"What's happened?" George Boardman asked. It was November of 1828, and he had been in Tavoy less than a year.

"Our chief's mother has died. He doesn't want the heathen funeral, because he has become a follower of Jesu Cree. But our people will perform the funeral ceremonies anyway. Our chief has told them to wait three more days because it's the cold season. Ko Thabew and his wife must come."

"We will go," said Thabew. He was ready to leave as soon as anyone came and asked. Quickly his wife gathered a few things for the journey.

The three moved so fast over the hills and through the underbrush that they barely had time to talk. They waded through icy rivers up to their armpits. They tried to sleep in the rain, covering themselves with their cloaks and some palm leaves.

"How many Christians are in your village now?" asked Thabew.

"Oh, many," answered the young man. "Since Moung So, the chief, and Apya Thi, the Keeper of the Book, trusted in Jesu Cree, many of us have believed in Him. But the air is full of fighting against us."

Thabew nodded. He knew it would be a fight. Not a fight of flesh and blood, but of spirits. The Holy Spirit on one side. The nats on the other. All the people who hadn't become Christians were still deathly afraid of the nats, especially when someone died. No wonder they still wanted to have a heathen funeral, even when the woman's son was a Christian.

On the third evening, when they arrived in the village of Chikku, they could hear the sound of wailing even from a distance.

"O dead one! O departed one!
Are you really gone?
Have you really left us?
We call, we cry out, but she cannot reply."

The drums of fear filled the surrounding hills as the three approached the village of Chikku.

They passed by a half-finished canoe. When the announcement of death had come, the man working on carving out that canoe had stopped his work. Now that canoe was cursed and would never be completed. All around were other projects that would be abandoned to the wild animals. Weaving that would never be finished. Traps that would never be made.

"Look, Ko Thabew, there is the body of Moung So's mother," said the young man who was their guide. Thabew nodded. He saw a crowd of people grouped around a hollowed-out log. Even without coming closer, he knew what was inside. The body of the dead woman would be all wrapped in cloths, so that no part showed.

Relatives came, one by one, placing at the head and at the foot of the hollowed trunk their gifts. Rice, a bowl of cooked jungle fowl, a cooking pot, a drinking cup.

The dead woman's old sister wailed, "O dead one! Eat, as when you were alive! Do not be ashamed!"

A friend cried out, "Oh! Oh! What is this! Now I am in the depths of sadness! In the past you spoke with me! Now you speak no more! Oh! Oh!"

"Come, dead ancestors!" called another. "Come and guide our sister to the land of the spirits of the dead!"

Then the mournful chant resumed, as the mourners danced slowly around the casket. Wailing, weeping, as those who have no hope.

"How we pity the dead!

We cannot awaken her."

Thabew and the others stood silently, watching. His wife said, "I remember when I was a girl. When my aunt died, they made me sing the whole funeral song."

Thabew could remember when he was a boy and his own uncle had died. As a teenager, he had participated in the funeral rites too. But now, his blood began to boil with his old rage. He felt his fists clenching in fury. *Those old nats! How they must be hopping in their laughter over all these Karens they've taken prisoner. That Mukawli! I hate him with all of my bones!*

As the people lit candles to continue their mourning into the twilight, into the darkness, the young man led the two visitors to the zayat they had built, not far from the funeral site. When they walked inside, the sight that Thabew saw warmed his heart so deeply that his anger melted away.

There, crouched together in a tightly-knit circle in the middle of the zayat, sat many who had become old familiar friends, maybe thirty or forty of them, men and women, old and young. There was Apya Thi, the old Keeper of the Book, with no more white robe, but dressed the same as others in a simple smock. There was Moung Kya. And there, in the middle, with tears streaming down his face, his face uplifted, his eyes closed and praying, crouched Moung So, the chief of the village. He whose mother's body now lay in a hollow tree.

For a moment the three newcomers stood respectfully. Then someone saw them. "They're here!" the whisper went through the group.

Moung So opened his eyes. "My brother!" His voice came out in a half sob. "My brother!" He leaped up and wrapped his arms around Thabew. "You've come. You can speak to us the Words of Life."

Outside, as the night fell, the mourners began to drink more and more alcohol and become more and more drunk. They began to yell and scream.

But inside, as Thabew's wife settled down next to the wife of Moung So, Thabew stood before the group and began to preach the Words of Life.

"Long ago Yuwah promised us that the Good Words would come in the white book!"

Moung So closed his eyes again and turned his face upwards. Tears began to stream down his face.

"We know that these good words have come to us now, and even more, the best Word of all is the Living Word, Jesu Cree, who spoke all the goodness of God to man."

The listeners began to rock back and forth, some with their eyes closed, some with their eyes fastened on the speaker. Outside the noises of the funeral grew louder, the wails and shrieks more piercing.

"He has given us His Holy Spirit!" Thabew cried out over the shrieks of the funeral. "His Holy Spirit is more powerful than the nats!"

Darkness gathered. Outside, the mourners lit torches to continue the funeral. Long mournful funeral dirges split the night, alternating with high shrieking singing. The torches moved about more wildly as the dancing became more fierce. The shrieks turned to wild laughter.

But inside the zayat, the small group of Christ-followers gathered even closer so they could hear each other without yelling. "We know that the Spirit of Jesu Cree is greater. Our people fear the nats. But we have no need to fear."

The next morning the funeral rites still hadn't ended. Thabew and his wife awoke to the smell of burning flesh. Moung So's mother's body was being burned. Through the day as the Christians prayed and sang and listened to Thabew's good words, they could still hear their relatives outside. They knew that they were taking one bone from the burned body, to bury it on the other side of the river.

> *"Clear the road,*
> *This mother will go forth,*
> *Mukawli has seized her;*
> *Black-winged Mukawli.*
> *We do not love to die,*
> *It makes us go insane;*
> *We do not love to leave this life;*
> *It makes us crazy.*
> *But to the place of the dead we will go.*
> *That the dead may arrive at her grave;*
> *The dead arrives today.*
> *Oh, spirit of our sister, return! Return!"*

In the zayat, Thabew struggled to read the Burmese New Testament so he could explain the truths in the Karen language. Sekyi worked with him to understand.

"Teacher Boardman told me that this is the part I should tell you about. Listen." He had the little New Testament opened to First Corinthians 15, where George had quickly marked some verses. Slowly and carefully Thabew tried to explain. "This is the way it is with the rising from the dead, like Jesu Cree. It goes down into the ground and rots. But it comes back up, and it is not rotten! It goes down and is ugly. It comes up and is beautiful! It goes down weak. It comes up strong! Now we look like this earth. But in the next life we will look like heaven! If we trust Jesus, we will one day be changed. So the grave and the fire and the nats will have no more victory. Their victory will be gone! Look! Listen! All our victory is in Christ Jesus!"

And while the chants and wailing and fire and moaning and shrieking laughter went on through the day from the hearts of the hopeless ones, the Christians listened to the voice and drank deep of the water of the Living Word of God.

See Thinking Further for Chapter 8 on page 139.

9. SLEEPLESS DELIGHT IN CHIKKU

George shielded his eyes from the tropical sun and sighed. "Through those mountains, Thabew?"

"Yes, on the other side," answered Thabew. "It will take only two more days."

It was February, 1829, and Teacher Boardman was taking that long-promised expedition to the village of Chikku, where Moung So was chief. He and his Karen friends had climbed for a full day, under the scorching sun, past rice fields, lonely huts and towering pagodas, through a jungle of bamboo, and past a caravan of elephant traders.

For a full day they had climbed, and then made camp in the rain—even though in this land of only two seasons, they had expected it to be dry. The rainy season was supposed to be over.

Now, on the second day of their three-day hike, for hour after hour they climbed. Thabew or one of the others often gave encouraging words to the missionary, whose face broke out in a sweat as he heaved his slim body over cliffs and precipices.

Down into the canyons, crossing the streams, and back up the other side. Past barren rice fields. Past groups of men beginning the chopping of a new grove of trees for the next rice field. On they went, on and on to the village of Moung So, the chieftain of Chikku.

Another night, this time in the home of some friendly Karens.

"What's the purpose of the bones everywhere, Ko Thabew?" Mr. Boardman asked. The bones of the jungle fowl lay in heaps, as if they had been collected.

"Teacher, this is how my people tell the future," Thabew explained in a low voice. "They read the bones and tell the people when they should plant, and which person is a witch, and what to do when someone is sick. This is what Mukawli told us to do."

George pondered. "Don't they seek answers from the true God, Yuwah?"

"No, Teacher. We told you that Yuwah is far from us and my people haven't known how to reach Him. This is what I've been preaching to my people. This is why you've come."

Every place they went, George observed the strange piles of bones of the jungle fowl, tall poles with skulls on them, and altars with pigs sacrificed on them. All of these things represented the hopeless prison of trying to understand the ways of Mukawli and the nats.

Hours later on the third day, they finally arrived at the village of Chikku, where Moung So was chief. This small settlement was as far east as a traveler could go before reaching Siam.

"Welcome, pale brother, welcome!" the men of the village called. Their faces beamed with joy. "You've come at last! We've long been waiting to see you!" They began to beat the big bronze drums to alert everyone in all the villages around. The big bronze drums boomed through the jungle air.

Soon people were flowing out of their huts, in that village and even in a few others, bringing ducks' eggs, yams, fish, fruit, jungle fowl, rice, and anything else they could find for a feast as important as this one—the feast that would welcome the long-awaited pale brother, who was finally bringing the truth of the great Yuwah back to the Karen people.

There was the huge zayat, built especially for the meetings the people of the village expected to have when the pale brother finally came. It was big enough to hold sixty or seventy people.

Thirty people from the village came that evening to hear Teacher Boardman speak in Burmese, as Thabew translated. Moung So, the chief, was very sick with a fever, but he wanted to hear the pale brother and his good words.

"For God so loved the world," George Boardman said, "that he gave His only Son." Thirty pairs of ears were opened to hear the words, first in Burmese, then in Karen. Thirty pairs of longing, searching eyes gazed at this pale brother.

Through the night many of them stayed and listened, longing to hear the truth. Moung So and Moung Kya seemed especially delighted. The words of their ancient prophets echoed in their ears.

> *The golden ship has arrived, has arrived!*
> *It has arrived with our younger brother!*
> *The worship that Yuwah appointed, the great worship,*
> *has reached the Karen people!*
> *Oh! Think about the great worship! We will be unable to sleep.*

The next morning was the Lord's Day. Early in the morning the people began to gather, men and women, old and children, about fifty of them, bringing gifts of food.

In Burmese, George preached, "Believe in the Lord Jesus, and you will be saved."

After he finished preaching, Thabew began to speak to the people in Karen. He told as much of Teacher Boardman's words as he could remember, and he added many words of his own.

George Boardman went away to pray, carrying with him *The Diary of David Brainerd*. He felt weak and empty. "Oh Lord," he prayed. "My love for You is so small. My focus on eternal things is so blurred. My grasp on Your great salvation is so poor. How can I be qualified to do this great work?"

But as he prayed, he remembered God saying to Paul, *"My power is made perfect in weakness."*

"O Lord God, You have given me a little love for the Karens. You have given me some eager desire for them to know You. O Lord, increase my faith, my love. Increase my passion for Your glory, and for the salvation of poor sinners."

After a time, George returned, where again fifty people were waiting for him to preach. This time he preached the words of Jesus, "Come to me, all who labor and are heavy laden."

In the evening he preached again, and again the people wanted to stay and stay.

Finally Teacher Boardman was ready to rest for the night. But there stood five men before him. There was Moung Kya, the one who had first desired to come find the pale foreigner at Tavoy. There was the chief, Moung So, who had resisted the heathen ceremonies when his mother died. There was Apya Thi, the Guardian of the Book. And two more.

Moung So bowed low. "Teacher Boardman. We believe all you've taught. We embrace Jesu Cree with all our hearts. We wish to be baptized in the Christian way."

* * *

After more than a year had passed, Sarah Boardman, George's wife, wrote a letter. She wrote, "The chief, Moung So, along with Moung Kya, take the booklets that we can give them and go from house to house, from village to village. In this way they preach the word and urge the people to believe on Jesus Christ. Their wives unite with them in fervent prayer, and worship with them on the Lord's Day. God is blessing their work. Many, many of their relatives have been baptized.

"Yes, my dear friend, the voice of prayer and praise rises sweetly from the dwellers on the desolate mountains of Southeast Asia."

See Thinking Further for Chapter 9 on page 139.

10. FAREWELL TO TEACHER BOARDMAN

Sau Quala watched the witch doctor hovering over his sick mother, whose eyes were closed in a fitful sleep. The witch doctor sprinkled blood on the mother's forehead and muttered, "We are offering the blood of this fowl. Go away and come not near." Then he sprinkled some water on her forehead and tied a yellow thread around her wrist. "Go away and come not near," he muttered again.

"Father." The seventeen-year-old young man spoke clearly, with only a slight tremor in his voice. "This is not the way of Yuwah."

The father jerked his head around and almost snarled in his anger. "Don't speak to me about your new religion! Since that Karen Christian came here there has been no peace!"

It had been a year since Thabew's first missionary trip—the one that lasted only four days because of the rain. But Sau Quala's house had been the very first one where he had stopped and proclaimed the good news of the coming of the Great Savior who had made the way to Yuwah.

As the witch doctor continued his mutterings, Sau Quala's mother opened her eyes and weakly raised her arm in protest. Her eyes met her son's in pleading.

Sau Quala turned his eyes away and stared at the dog skull, stuck on the end of a pole at the door of their hut. How could he speak to his father? Of course his "new religion" was really no new religion. It was the fulfillment of the ancient way of Yuwah, the way they had been anticipating for generations.

No peace? In his own heart, in his mother's heart, there had entered great peace. It was only in the life of his father that Sau Quala saw no peace.

"Mother," he whispered. "You and father named me Sau Quala, which means hope. Now you and I know that our hope is only in Jesu Cree. That truth is what I will follow."

He walked out, with determination in his heart. The next time the pale foreigner came through his village, he would receive baptism. He loved the true God and His Son Jesus Christ. He would identify himself as a Christian.

* * *

Just a year later in February of 1831, Sau Quala stood with his father—who was now a joyful new Christian himself—and listened to the pale Teacher for the last time. Only thirty years old, only his third trip to the mountains, but George Boardman was dying of consumption.

Mr. Francis Mason and his wife had recently joined the Boardmans at Tavoy. Now, he and many Karen men had trekked through the hills, carrying the pale Teacher on his bed all the way to the foot of the mountain next to the stream. Sarah Boardman had also come, because she feared that her husband would die before he returned home.

"How are you, Teacher?" Sau Quala asked anxiously.

"Better than I had hoped," George Boardman answered weakly. He raised up and smiled at the Karens, over a hundred of them, gathered to hear him speak, and to request baptism. His voice sounded feeble. "I'm much encouraged to see this gathering of Karens who all want to hear the Word of God and identify themselves with our great Savior in baptism."

Mrs. Boardman spoke hopefully. "Maybe this beautiful spot, surrounded by your beloved Karens, will strengthen you."

Day after day the Karens drank in the words that Mr. Mason and Teacher Boardman, even in his weak state, spoke to them. They couldn't get enough of the truths of the great God and His Son, Jesus Christ.

George spoke with the many women and old men who were asking for baptism. But his strength was growing weaker and weaker.

"Oh, Mr. Boardman," said his wife, "don't you think we should go back to Tavoy where you can rest and be cared for?"

At this, the young missionary raised up. With bright eyes in his sallow, sunken face he said, "Sarah, the cause of God is more important than my health, and if I return now, our whole purpose in coming will be defeated. I want to see the work of the Lord go on." He fell back on his bed.

"Sarah," he gasped. "What if my life is cut short because we stay? Does that mean I should leave? Shouldn't I help gather in these precious lambs of God? Sarah, you knew before we came that coming to a foreign field could mean that either of our lives might be cut short. But we wanted to obey the Lord. And we have compassion for these heathen who are perishing because they haven't heard the Good News of Christ. This is why we've made this sacrifice. Sarah, we've never been sorry that we came. No, we praise God that He brought us to Burma, and to Tavoy, and to the base of this mountain."

Sau Quala watched as Teacher Boardman's bright eyes focused on his wife with a look of tenderness. "My love. I can't live long. If we go home now, I'll miss this most important work of the baptism of so many souls. Then at home, I'll last only a few more days and be gone. What would the value be, as I remember that I missed this most important work out here in the wilderness in order to have a few days more of idle life? So you see that I must stay until the Karens are baptized."

Then Teacher Boardman looked up to Mr. Mason and smiled with radiance. "If I can live to see this baptism, this evidence of God's work, then I'll feel a special outpouring of mercy. I'll be like Simeon and say, 'Lord, now let Your servant depart in peace, for my eyes have seen Your salvation!' "

A little before sunset that evening, Sau Quala and others helped to carry Teacher Boardman on his bed out to the riverbank for the baptisms. The pale Teacher lifted his heavy head to gaze on the scene, where Mr. Mason baptized thirty-four new Karen Christians, most of them women. They came up from the water with their smocks and their long black hair flowing with water. Their faces shone brightly, and they lifted their arms and their faces to heaven.

After supper, about fifty new Karen Christians gathered with Sau Quala around Teacher Boardman to listen to him one last time. "God is calling me home," he said weakly. "Soon I'll be eternally happy with Him in heaven. When I'm gone, remember what I taught you. Listen to these teachers. Pray, obey, and trust the eternal, unchangeable God. Earthly teachers sicken and die, but God remains forever the same. Love Jesus Christ with all your hearts, and you will be forever safe."

With sober faces and tears, the Karen Christians promised that they would.

The next morning the loving Karens carefully carried George Boardman to a boat that they could steer down the river most of the way to Tavoy to take him back to his home. Mr. Mason and Sarah Boardman climbed on after him.

Suddenly they realized that he was breathing his last. His bright eyes stared, unseeing.

"Oh, come! Come!" Sarah called. The Karens waded into the river to gather around him, to watch his last gentle breathings as he passed through death into eternal life.

"O Yuwah," prayed Sau Quala. "Our Teacher is gone to You. He is the one who showed us the way to You, the way to be happy forever. Thank you for bringing us this great Teacher. Take him happily into Your great place." Sau Quala and others, when they watched him die trusting in Jesus Christ, were changed forever.

"Teacher Mason," said Sau Quala. "I will live with you. I want to better understand the way of Jesu Cree."

Over the course of the year, more and more Karens came to Mr. Mason. "I want to believe in Jesu Cree. I heard of Him from Teacher Boardman."

* * *

Sau Quala, whose name was Hope, came to be called Teacher Hope. Like Thabew, he traveled from village to village proclaiming the truth of the Gospel of Jesus Christ.

See Thinking Further for Chapter 10 on page 140.

11. MISSIONARY TO THE WILD MEN

T ime rolled on. For years Francis Mason spent almost all his time working in his study with Sau Quala and other language helpers, trying to understand the Karen language, trying get the New Testament translated for the Karen Christians who were begging to have the White Book in their own language. Six years after he arrived, in 1837, he finally had the first New Testament book translated, the book of Matthew. The Karens rejoiced. They learned to read. They grew in their faith and understanding.

In 1843, Mr. Mason finished translating the New Testament. Ten years after that, in 1853, he finished the Old. The Karens read and taught. Pastors arose from their midst, and more Karen missionaries went out to their own people.

And now, almost fifty years had passed since Thabew, the "Karen Apostle," had received the gospel from Adoniram Judson and George Boardman and had begun taking it to all his countrymen. More than twenty thousand

Karen Christians now gathered in zayats throughout their villages to sing praises to God and to hear the Bible read in their very own language. They lifted their hands, they clapped, they sang to rejoice in the great salvation of Jesus Christ.

And now it was time for the Annual Assembly! The rainy season had ended, the harvests had been gathered. Karen Christians from the village schools, young and old, all through the surrounding hills, donned their brightest and cleanest clothes, the silk clothes that they had made themselves from the cocoons of the silkworms, to bring their harvest to the big meeting place.

They came, laden down with beautiful flowers and baskets full of food. Baskets overflowing with rice and all kinds of luscious fruits. They brought sweet potatoes, millet, squashes, eggplant, and tender young bamboo shoots. Baskets of delicious fried grasshoppers and locusts and ants and snails. Eels and snakes, deer and peacocks to roast, and even a buffalo.

They came across the hills singing. They came to the largest zayat some of them had ever seen—big enough to hold over fifteen hundred people! They came to sing and feast with all the other Christians and to listen to preaching from the pale missionaries and their own leaders.

And they came to pray for those among them who had still not yet been reached.

One speaker pointed to a large map of the Karen Hills. "We see here that the tribes on the west side of the watershed have been reached with the gospel. But on the other side of the watershed is the Brec tribe."

A murmur went through the crowd. Everyone knew about the Brec tribe. They ate raw meat and drank blood. They wore no clothes. They killed people just for fun. One of the Christian missionaries, Saw Aw, had lost his wife and child to these cruel robbers.

The Christians had wanted to reach them, had prayed to reach them. But the Christians were afraid.

"Can't we send someone to this tribe?" the speaker asked. "Has God called someone to this tribe?"

But there was silence. Everyone wanted the gospel to go to the Brecs. But they wanted someone else to take it.

Off to the side sat Su Yah, who had come to Christ under the teachings of Teacher Hope. When he was young he had left for Bible School. Then he and his wife took Christ to a village that had never heard the gospel, and they stayed there for years. Then to another village. Now Su Yah was in middle age, and held the position of secretary of this great Assembly.

Su Yah bowed his head in prayer. But he prayed only briefly.

"I'll go," he said, standing. "My heart is heavy for these poor Brecs. They don't know Yuwah or His great love, and no one wants to go to them. If my church will grant me permission, I'll go."

The leader stood up, as the others gazed at Su Yah in surprise. "Su Yah will go!" he cried out. "Let's pray!" All bowed their heads. "O, our mighty Yuwah, You who made all things, You who poured out Your love on us through Your Son Jesu Cree! You have given great power to Su Yah to take the Good News to a people who have never heard! You have filled Su Yah with Your love! Go with him!"

When the meeting had dismissed, other Karen Christians gathered around Su Yah. "How can you do this?" they asked. "Don't you remember that Saw Aw never saw his wife and child again?"

"I'll go alone," said Su Yah. "My wife and children will stay behind."

"But the way is so long, full of tigers and bears and snakes and wild elephants. And, if you get there, the Brecs may kill you before you can even say a word."

"When I was young, God delivered me from a bear, and He delivered me from a tiger. He'll be with me in this work. I will go."

After the Assembly had ended, when Su Yah and his family had returned to their village, he kissed his wife and children, leaving them in the care of his church. With his

Bible and his hymn book, he began to walk from village to village in the direction of the Brecs.

For a while, others walked with him. But then he came to the edge of Burma. The others went back. But Su Yah kept walking, up and up and up, over a high mountain, covered with thick, dark green forests.

At the very top of the mountain, six thousand feet high, Su Yah looked out to the east. This was the watershed. The river on one side flowed to the Andaman Sea. On the other it flowed into the Gulf of Siam. Down there somewhere, on the other side of this mountain, were the Brecs.

Su Yah lifted his hands to the sky and prayed. "I know, O Yuwah, that my life may end at any moment. I know that when I see the Brecs, they may kill me before I can speak. But my life is Yours, and if this is the way my life ends, what better way for my life to come to You? I will come singing."

Mountain peaks loomed before him at every turn. Valleys yawned at the bottom, as deep and dark as canyons.

Here and there in the distance, Su Yah could see the smoke from village fires. These must be the fires of the Brec people. Once again the missionary gathered his bag, his Bible, and his hymn book, and began to work his way down the mountain.

And so, before too long, there he was at the edge of a village. This was the village of Letcho, where some of the terrible Brec people lived. Scattered around on the ground lay dead animals covered with flies, chicken bones placed in careless piles, crude bowls full of blood with maggots floating on top.

"Augh! A stranger!" The women and children, wild hair flying, screamed and ran into their huts.

"An enemy! Kill him!" cried the men. "A spy! Kill him!" They grabbed their spears and knives and ran toward Su Yah.

But Su Yah stood quietly. He didn't even look afraid.

The Brec warriors, in their confusion, stopped yelling. They stood trembling, their filthy rags hanging in tatters on their filthy bodies.

"Look!" said Su Yah as soon as they were quiet. "I have no spear. Do I look like a man of war?" He held up his Bible and his hymn book. "Do these look like an enemy's weapons?"

The men stood silent, their spears still poised, their knives still thrust forward. But they listened.

See Thinking Further for Chapter 11 on page 140.

12. WILD MEN CLEAR THE WAY

Su Yah held the book high. "This is the White Book!" he cried. "This is the Book of which our ancestors spoke, from days long ago!" Then he opened the book and turned the white, white pages. "Listen to the Book speak." He read from the very beginning of the Book and then translated to the Brec dialect. "In the beginning, Yuwah made all things, the sky and the earth."

The savage men, with their bloodshot eyes, stared at Su Yah.

Then Su Yah began to sing. His deep, beautiful voice rang through the mountains, and the Brecs all stared. Even the women and children peered out from the huts. No one here had ever heard anyone sing.

"Happy day!" Su Yah sang in the Brec dialect. "Happy day that took my heart to You, my Savior and my God."

Su Yah sang and sang. He saw what the song was doing to the hearts of these men—and to their hands.

The hands holding the spears and knives fell lower and lower, until the spears had dropped on the ground and the knives had returned to their sheaths.

"It is well, it is well with my soul," Su Yah sang. And he knew it was. The love of Jesus Christ filled his heart. He loved these dirty, smelly, ignorant wild savages. He loved these people who might still kill him at any moment. His heart was filled with the love of God.

When the song had ended, one man grunted one word. "More." So Su Yah sang again. And again and again, through the afternoon and into the evening. The men sat down on the ground. The woman and children crept out of the huts.

Then Su Yah spoke. "I have come," he said, "to bring you the important message from the great Yuwah, the one who gave us the white Book. It is a message of hope."

"He is like Saw Aw," muttered the chief, a huge man with broad shoulders and a big knife.

"Do you know Saw Aw?" Su Yah asked. How well he remembered the story of Saw Aw's wife and child being taken away, never to be seen again.

"We have heard of him and his words," replied the chief. "He is old, but he has lived with another tribe for many years. He helps the sick and the poor."

"We heard about a man that the witch doctor could not cure," said another. "But Saw Aw used a white powder and made him well."

"A Brec man took Saw Aw's wife and child," said the chief. "But he still helps people. You are like him."

For days Su Yah stayed and proclaimed the Gospel of Jesus Christ, to this village and three others nearby. "Your life of violence and crime will only bring you destruction!" he preached. "Yuwah has been patient with you because you didn't know Him. But now that you know of Him, you must repent!"

Su Yah pointed to the piles of chicken bones, to the rotting nat sacrifices. "Don't you see that the nats have never helped you? You sacrifice to them, but you still never have enough to eat! You still barely stay alive! You still always live in fear!"

In their hearts, the Brecs knew he was right. Many of them listened hungrily when he read to them from the white Book.

For weeks Su Yah stayed. But finally he shouldered his bag and gathered his book. "I must return to my family. But you will see me again. Remember the words I have told you."

* * *

It was time again for the Annual Assembly. Everyone had heard that Su Yah had spent weeks with the murderous Brec tribe and had touched their hearts with the Gospel of Jesus Christ. Everyone was eager to come and hear more about what had happened.

But even as the Christians were gathering from all over, they were caught by surprise.

There, over the hills, marched a team of wild men, armed as if for battle, with crude shields and spears and drums and horns.

The wild men approached from a distance, up hills and down. As they banged on their drums and blared their horns, as they pounded their spears in time with

their walking and smacked their shields and whooped, some of the Christians began to quail in fear.

"Don't fear," said Su Yah confidently. "It's the Brecs. I think they come in peace."

When the tribe finally reached the Assembly grounds, the chief stepped forward. This was the huge chief with broad shoulders. "I am Ho Wi," he said. He gazed around the crowd of Christians boldly.

But then he saw Su Yah. "My brother!" he cried. Suddenly all the Brec warriors who had followed him began to rattle their shields and beat their drums and shriek, all in greeting to Su Yah.

With great noise and fanfare, the Brecs seated themselves in the meeting. They listened to the children singing, and their listening wasn't quiet. They beat their drums and called out their approval.

They marveled loudly at the building, the largest building they had ever seen. They listened to the teaching, but understood little. They wondered that people could sit still for so long, or walk in such neat rows.

The next day, at the Assembly, Su Yah made his mission report. And there, sitting among the other Christians, were the people he had gone to as a missionary!

"My brothers and sisters," Su Yah began, "I'm sure that all of us can remember a time when our fathers and mothers, and perhaps even our very own lives, were trapped in darkness, believing that Yuwah was far away and could not be reached. The best news of all is that *He is Near*. He has come Near to us through His own Son, Jesu Cree! A year ago I left you to take this news to the Brec tribe. I didn't care if I lost my life. What better way to lose one's life?"

Here, Su Yah pointed to the chief, Ho Wi. "Here is the man who first received me in the village of Letcho, Chief Ho Wi. He is here to learn more about who Jesu Cree is and how he can trust in Him."

At this point, Ho Wi stood and spoke in the Brec dialect. As he spoke, Su Yah translated. "I came," said the chief, "because when Su Yah brought the Good Words to us, much good came to our people. We had no thought of living any other way than the way we had lived for all the ages, except that we had heard stories about the kindness of Saw Aw. We couldn't understand it. But Su Yah told us about the kindness of God through Jesu Cree. Now we want Su Yah to return and live with us again."

Ho Wi lifted his spear. "We are weary of trying to keep the nats from hurting us," he said. "We live in fear. We want Yuwah to be our King, to live in hope. He loves and cares for His children. We want to follow and obey Him."

Ho Wi turned to the pale teacher with the bright red beard, Alonzo Bunker. "If the pale teacher will come," he said, "my people will believe."

The pale teacher pulled his handkerchief out of his pocket and wiped his eyes. He remembered praying with Su Yah the year before, wondering if he was sending him to his death.

"Yes, we will gladly come," he said.

"We have prepared the way for you," said Ho Wi. "We've cut a road from the top of the mountain to our villages. We've brushed away all the leaves. We've placed bamboos of water along the side for you. My people will come to meet us with food."

"You have prepared the way of the Lord," Alonzo murmured, "just as John the Baptist said. And the Lord will come."

See Thinking Further for Chapter 12 on page 141.

13. THE END OF THE REIGN OF THE NATS

With great excitement, Mr. and Mrs. Bunker and their two little girls, Su Yah with his wife and children, and many other Karen Christians made ready for the journey to Letcho, the village of the Brecs. A few days later they started out in a long caravan.

They climbed over huge mountains. Down and down, and across the swift-running streams. Through the forests that were so thick the sunlight was shut out. Single file they walked, sixty of them, with Su Yah in the lead.

On the third day they came to the very top of the watershed mountain, where they could see the glorious vista. One mountain after another lay before their eyes. Valley after valley.

"So beautiful!" one of the little girls exclaimed.

"It is beautiful," said her mother. "But just think, when Su Yah first came here, God wasn't looking at the beautiful view. He was looking at the beautiful feet.

'How beautiful upon the mountains are the feet of him who brings good news, who publishes salvation!' "

The way down from the top of the mountain was much easier. Ho Wi had received word that the missionary team was coming, and he left his village to greet them. True to his word, he had worked hard with his men to clear the way.

"You didn't even know the Scripture, Ho Wi," observed Alonzo, "but you wanted to prepare the way of the Lord and make straight in the desert a highway for our God."

Ho Wi looked at him quizzically. "I wanted you to come and give the Good Words," he said simply. "Look! My young men are coming! Sit! Sit!" There, coming toward them on the path, were a dozen young men with baskets of cooked rice for everyone to eat.

Finally, at twilight, the group of weary travelers passed around a huge bluff with a sparkling waterfall and suddenly arrived at Letcho, the small Brec village where a few new believers eagerly waited to hear about Jesu Cree.

Along the village path, and throughout the village itself, the visitors saw tall poles crowned with ox skulls from the sacrifices, placed there to scare away the nats.

But Ho Wi's villagers had never seen a pale foreigner before, and had no idea that people with bright red hair even existed.

"Ah hie! Ah hie!" they screamed. Once again, some of them ran for their lives. Some just stared, with open mouths. Then the dogs began to bark and the pigs to squeal.

But Ho Wi came up and began to speak. "This is our brother!" he said, pointing to Su Yah. "These are our friends!" and he opened his arm expansively to include all the pale foreigners and all the boys and girls who had come to carry their baggage.

At Ho Wi's introduction, the Brec people began to emerge from inside their huts and behind the trees. They touched the pale strangers' shoes and clothes. They touched the little girls' hair. "Oh, oh! Are they real?"

The next day Ho Wi took Su Yah and Alonzo to see the zayat his people had built. "See, my brothers," he said, "this is the place for you to tell us the Good Words."

95

"Come to listen!" someone called. "Listen to the words of Su Yah and the pale foreigner!"

They began to beat on their bronze drums. All the people came, hundreds of them, in great excitement. They had never been to such a meeting. To them, it seemed like a festival. So they gathered around the stand, talking, laughing, smoking, dancing, drinking, and playing. Finally Su Yah and Alonzo managed to make them be quiet and listen. Then Alonzo spoke, and Su Yah translated.

"Men and women! I see you have here many sacrifices to the nats. You have sacrificed oxen to Mukawli. You have placed ox skulls on poles everywhere to scare away the nats.

"I have a question for you. Does it work? Have you scared away the nats? No! Because Mukawli took your fathers and mothers prisoner long ago. You dare not make any decision without studying the bird bones. You never know when Mukawli will strike one of you with sickness and death. He holds you in a prison of fear."

All voices were silent. All eyes gazed at him. They knew what he said was true.

"Mukawli is the father of lies. He lies to you and says, 'Oh, Yuwah cannot be reached. He has gone far away and will never come back.'

"But I tell you that Yuwah is near! It is your own sin that keeps you from Him. But Jesu Cree has come to bear your sin for you and make the way to Yuwah!"

As Su Yah translated, he watched the faces of the Brec people. The pale foreigner was teaching the same truths that he himself had taught when he lived with the Brecs.

"We saw when we came that you had cleared the way for us," Alonzo continued. "We thank you very much for that."

The Brecs murmured their delight that their hard work had been noticed.

"But now Yuwah says, 'Clear the way for Me! Clear away the wrong thinking and the nat appeasement! Clear the way in your hearts and your heads for the coming of Jesu Cree!' "

Before many days had passed, Ho Wi and several of the elders came to Su Yah and Alonzo. "We want to enter the new religion," Ho Wi said. "Yuwah is more powerful than all the nats. The nats are bad, and liars; we can never trust them. Yuwah is good and speaks truth. We believe this, and we will worship Him."

The other elders nodded in agreement. But all of them looked wide-eyed with fear.

"This is great news!" said Alonzo. "Why do you look fearful?"

"We fear the nats," Ho Wi explained. "If we destroy our nat worship now, they will take revenge on us. You are already in Jesu Cree, and the nats cannot harm you. Will you destroy our nat worship for us now?"

"We will do it!" cried Su Yah. "Come, boys and girls!" The Karen boys and girls who had come with the missionaries gathered from every part of the village where they were playing. While the fearful Brec people watched, the Karen Christians, without fear, began to knock down poles of ox skulls, break down crude stone altars, carry away bowls of rotten blood, gather up piles of bird bones and baskets of rotten eggs. The villagers watched, quaking with fear.

Ho Wi and the other elders gazed in awe. The nats wouldn't take revenge?

Even the little girls, the daughters of the pale foreigners, grabbed the vines that the Brecs believed were stairs for the nats to climb to the tops of the trees where they lived. When one little girl took a knife to the vine, the Brecs cried out, "The nat will surely kill her!" But when the vine fell to the ground, and she turned back to the crowd, they exclaimed, "Yuwah is surely stronger than the nats!"

"Here!" cried the people now, gaining courage. "Take this! And this!" They gathered one sacrifice and magic charm after another. As the young men made a huge pile in the middle of the village, Su Yah got a torch to build a great bonfire.

"What about the banyan tree?" someone said, pointing. All eyes turned to the giant tree on the far edge of the village. The air roots dropped down to make new trunks, and throughout the tree were spread sacrifices and charms, to appease and confuse the banyan demon that held the people in fear.

"Yes, the banyan!" said another. "Will you take the banyan?"

One of the missionaries took a knife and strode to the tree with confidence. As each branch fell, a cheer arose from the crowd.

"Yah!" they cried. "Yuwah is full of power!"

"Yah!" they cried. "We are free from the nats! We will worship Yuwah!"

When it was finally time for the missionaries to leave, Su Yah said, "My family and I will stay, brother. I remember what the Lord said in Isaiah. 'He hath sent me to bind up the brokenhearted, to proclaim liberty to the captives, and the opening of the prison to those who are bound.' "

A few years later, Letcho was home to a church of forty strong, baptized members. Many other villages of the Brecs also heard the gospel through Su Yah and started their own churches too.

See Thinking Further for Chapter 13 on page 141.

14. A BATTLE OF THE SPIRITS

Chief Tippeh uttered the words like a snarl. "Those Christians in that Brec village! They have pulled others to their side. Now the only reason they prosper is because they have help from the pale missionaries!"

"But the pale missionaries haven't been here in eight years!" protested one of the men. "They prosper because they have forsaken the nats and worship Yuwah."

"They prosper because they have stopped raiding other villages and live in peace," observed another man. "And we've been afraid to attack, because they have Yuwah on their side."

"Well, let us no longer be afraid to attack," growled the chief. "We've raided all the villages around here, until there's nothing left to raid. But that prosperous village of the Christians—they have plenty!"

"But the Christian God is nothing like the nats or the idols of the Burmans!" argued one of the warriors. "The Christian God protects His people!"

"No, the chief is right," said another warrior. "We can attack that Brec village that first turned to this new Way, that village of Letcho. Then, if we win, we'll know that the Christian God is a dead God like the gods of the Burmans. Then we can quickly destroy all the Christian villages."

The men who supported Chief Tippeh's idea won out over the ones who feared. The village set up their plan to attack Letcho, the very first Brec village where people believed in Jesus Christ.

"We will study the bones of the jungle fowl to find the best time to start out against them," muttered the chief. And all the men agreed.

But somehow word came to the village of Letcho that the enemies of Yuwah were planning a raid against them.

"What will we do?" asked Ho Wi, the chief. "It's wrong for us to fight with weapons of war. If we fight with weapons, we're saying we believe Yuwah isn't strong enough to defend us."

"Yes," agreed Su Yah. "And if we kill them, they'll die in their sins and have no chance to believe on Jesu Cree." He stopped to think. "Here's how we'll fight," he said. "I'll write letters to all the pastors and all the elders around the Hill Tribes. I'll ask everyone to pray, and to continue to pray. This is a battle of the spirits. It must be fought with weapons of the Spirit."

"Will we be afraid?" Ho Wi asked his people.

"No!" some of them answered. But others looked at him with large eyes. What if Yuwah didn't protect them? They would all be dead.

"Will He help us as He helped His people in the Bible?" asked one small voice. It was a little boy.

"Will He help us as He helps the pale foreigners?" echoed the boy's mother.

"Our God is great," said Saw Aw, who had suffered the loss of his wife and child. "And our God is good. We will trust Him."

Every day, day after day, the village of Letcho gathered for prayer. "O Yuwah," they cried, "show Yourself strong to the other villages of the Brecs." They wanted to pray in faith, not fear. But some of them were afraid.

One morning it happened.

"My son!" cried a Christian mother.

"My son!" cried another.

Two little boys had been kidnapped. Even now the Christians could see the enemy tribesmen running down the hill to the rushing river.

"Come back!" Some of the men chased after them. But the enemy warriors were prepared. They quickly crossed the rushing, swollen stream in a boat that other warriors were holding ready. The men of Letcho couldn't follow quickly enough.

The battle of the spirits had begun. Who would win? The two mothers were sobbing. The two fathers looked grim and reached for their spears.

Though Su Yah had been a pastor for years, and a Christian for even more years than that, he still knew how powerful the nats were. He knew this was a battle of the spirits. "Oh my brother," Su Yah said to Saw Aw. "When I was young, I killed a bear—it took six men to carry his body back to my village. I would rather face another bear like that one than these enemies of the spirit. If we could gather weapons and go against them, we could get those little boys back. But oh, now we must just be still and pray and love our enemies!"

The Christians gathered around the two elders, looking at each other soberly. Could they really simply wait for Yuwah to do His work? Wouldn't their boys be killed?

"Don't be discouraged," said Saw Aw. "Yuwah will fight for us. He will make His Name great in the enemy villages. We must not go against them with weapons of war. We must go against them with the prayer of faith!"

Again the Christian leaders wrote letters to all the pastors in the Hill Tribes. "Please come to Letcho and pray with us for God to bring back these two boys and show Himself strong to the heathen villages!"

The pastors came from the other Christian villages. And not only the pastors, but many Christians from the other villages came too. More and more and more, until hundreds of them had gathered for prayer at Letcho.

"We know that this is a battle of the Spirit!" Saw Aw cried out. "We'll cry out to Yuwah! We'll remember His promises! We'll seek His wisdom!"

For days they prayed, crying out to God to release the boys, crying out for wisdom.

Finally they knew what to do. A group of men would walk the day's journey to the enemy village, and demand release of the two boys. They would be like Moses, telling Pharaoh to let God's people go. Surely God would accomplish this work.

Several men volunteered. They marched into the enemy camp, trusting God. "In the Name of the great God, Yuwah!" they exclaimed. "The living God, the God over all, we demand the return of the two boys you stole!"

But just like Pharaoh, Chief Tippeh refused. "You didn't bring ransom money?" he sneered at them. "Why should I let them go? You can pay me three hundred rupees apiece, or you can come and fight! I will not let your children go."

The chief didn't tell them that many people in his village heard the demand with quaking hearts. They feared the living God. They were afraid to hurt the two little boys, for fear of what the living God might do to them.

The men of Letcho returned to their village, heavy-hearted, not knowing what was happening in the enemy village. What should they do? They couldn't pay a ransom—that would show Yuwah to be weak. They couldn't go to war.

On hearing the distressing news, some of the Christians in Letcho became faint-hearted. But one old man arose.

"Young men," he cried out, "how many times did the Israelites march around Jericho before its walls fell?"

The men of the committee looked at him as if this were a new thought. "Seven times," said one.

"How many times did Elijah pray for rain before it came?"

"Seven times."

"And Moses had to go to Pharaoh many times too!" added another. "And we've demanded the return of our captives only once!"

A murmur of excitement began to move through the crowd. All the Christians from all the visiting villages knew that they were engaged in a spiritual battle just as important for them as the battles of the Spirit had been for the ancient Israelites, or the early Christians.

"Who will go this time to demand the return of the boys in the Name of our great Yuwah?" asked Su Yah.

A new Rescue Committee volunteered and trekked for a day to the enemy village.

"In the Name of the great Yuwah, the living God, the God over all!" they cried out. "We demand that you give us the boys you stole!"

Once again Chief Tippeh refused. "Let Yuwah come Himself and we will give them up!" he said. "If you come again without ransom money, we will kill you!"

But this time the Letcho men didn't seem downcast or discouraged. They said not a word, but turned to leave.

As soon as they were gone, the chief's wife came out of her hut. "Give them the children!" she insisted. "Their Yuwah will destroy us all! I fear Him!"

But like Pharaoh, the chief's heart was hard, and he refused. "If Yuwah Himself appears," he said, "then I will give up the boys. After all, we're keeping them safe. Just in case Yuwah really does appear."

See Thinking Further for Chapter 14 on page 141.

15. SINGING THE BATTLE

The Christians weren't discouraged. "What now? What does the Spirit of Yuwah want us to do?" They were ready to go back five more times, or more if they needed to.

Strengthened in the Spirit, they decided to move their prayer meeting a day's journey away, just outside the village where the stolen boys were held captive. Scores and scores of Christians settled outside Tippeh's village and continued to pray. For three days they prayed, while the people of the enemy village became more and more frightened.

On the third day, a message came from Tippeh. "If Chief Ho Wi and the parents of the boys will come into my village," the messenger recited, "we will give you the captive boys."

"Yuwah has answered our prayer!" rejoiced some of the Christians.

But Ho Wi's response was different. "Brothers," he said, "I know that this chief is a cunning man. He will lay an ambush for us and take us all captive too. I won't go."

"But surely this is an answer to our prayer!" cried out some. And so through the night they argued and prayed and discussed and prayed and talked and prayed.

"Who will go?"

Su Yah arose. "I will go."

Saw Aw arose. "I will go."

The father of one of the boys arose. "I will go."

A deacon of one of the other Christian villages arose. "I will go."

Though it was still dark, the small group lit torches and walked through the dark forest. Though they knew Tippeh had said he would kill them if they came without money, they pressed on.

At daylight the Christian men entered the village. "Awoo!" The dogs began to howl, signaling their approach.

"An enemy army!" the women shrieked, and grabbing their children, they ran into the jungle.

Tippeh's men gathered quickly, holding their spears and shields. But they trembled.

But the men of Letcho held no weapons. All they held were books, books with white pages. Tippeh and his men stared.

Calmly, and filled with the power of the Holy Spirit, Su Yah said, "Let us sing hymn number 124." The men of Letcho turned in their hymn books and began to sing their translation of a great hymn by Charles Wesley.

"Father, I stretch my hands to You! No other help I know;
If You withdraw Yourself from me, ah! where then shall I go?"

They sang for their lives, as the men of Tippeh's village stared at them, their spears outstretched.

"What did Your only Son endure, before I drew my breath?
What pain, what labor, to secure my soul from endless death?"

The women and children edged back from the jungle at this strange and beautiful sound.

"O Jesus, if I could believe, now I would feel Your power;
Now my poor soul You would retrieve, nor let me wait one hour."

The enemy warriors laid their spears on the ground. Some of them squatted to listen.

"Author of faith! to You I lift My weary, longing eyes:
O let me now receive that gift! My soul without it dies."

The enemy warriors stood or squatted motionless, as if spellbound. Their eyes were large and their mouths hung open. They had never seen warfare like this.

"The worst of sinners would rejoice, could they but see Your face:
O, let me hear Your quickening voice, and taste Your
pardoning grace."

The last notes of the beautiful song echoed through the village. Then Su Yah spoke. "Let us pray!"

Su Yah's companions fell to their knees. Together they beseeched Yuwah, as Su Yah cried out in prayer. "Our great and mighty Father, Yuwah!" he cried. "You have opened our blind eyes! You have softened our hard hearts! I cry out for You to do the same for the people of this heathen village! I cry out to you for this hard-hearted chief, Tippeh! I pray that he will not call down on himself Your judgment!"

Su Yah opened his eyes and stood, gazing on the trembling warriors.

"Sit down, all of you," he commanded.

The warriors sat. Tippeh sat, staring at Su Yah in fear.

"I bring you a message from Yuwah, the living God," said Su Yah. "You heard us sing words you have never heard before. This living God, Yuwah, is one we call Father. We stretch out our hands to Him, and He helps us. Through the great sacrifice of His only Son, Jesu Cree, we know the great blessings of happiness and peace in Him. We have known the gift of His Holy Spirit, who makes us strong!

"But what do you have? Fear and war and poverty! No blessings from the Living God! Turn to Him and repent and cry out to Him for pardon!"

Tippeh, the hard-faced old chief, had crept closer and closer to Su Yah as he spoke. His face began to soften with longing.

When Su Yah ceased speaking, Tippeh said quietly. "Take your boys. Take them back to your village."

At these words, some women came out of a hut with the two little boys, who quickly ran to the men. The Christian father had thought he might never see his little boy again. What joy!

The news spread rapidly to all the villages around. Kidnappers had returned their victims without ransom, without war! The only weapons were prayer and song! Surely the God of the Christians was a mighty God!

Tippeh's village and then over twenty other villages, sent messages to the Christians. "Send us teachers. We want to become followers of Jesu Cree."

See Thinking Further for Chapter 15 on page 142.

16. THE VILLAGE OF LONG-NECKS

Alonzo Bunker shaded his eyes and looked up. "It looks like maybe two hundred more feet of climbing to get to that village," he said. He gazed out at the Karen children and teenagers who had come with them, playing among the rocks as if they were mountain goats. They didn't need to rest, but they were happy to play while the pale teacher rested.

Alonzo wiped his brow and looked down to the stream winding its way around the bottom of the cliff. "We've probably already come one or two hundred feet. I just can't believe they built their village so high up. It seems nearly impossible."

"Not impossible, you know, Teacher," said Tio, the Karen missionary. "The women have to haul water from that stream down there almost every day."

Alonzo shook his head. "To think that they could be so violent that they have to protect themselves like this." He pulled up his pants leg and studied his knees, torn and bruised from climbing on the rocks to this cave. "I hope they'll listen to the Gospel."

"The Gospel of Jesu Cree is for all of us," said Tio. "I lived in ignorance until I heard. And Teacher," he continued, "even though you're from the land across the water, I think you lived in ignorance until you heard too."

"That I did," Alonzo agreed. "My ignorance looked different from this, but it was ignorance, all the same." He paused and considered. "My own ancestors, back in Europe, offered human sacrifices."

"Look, Teachers!" one of the children called, pointing down. There near the bottom of the cliff, climbing on the narrow, rocky path with sure feet and one hand, came the women of the Lennite village. In the other hand, balanced on one shoulder, they carried jugs of water and loads of wood.

But it wasn't the heavy loads that made Alonzo stare. It was their necks. "What are they wearing?" he gasped.

"Those are their neck rings," answered Tio. "The Padaung women have worn them for longer than anyone can remember."

"They look terrible!" exclaimed one of the children. "The women look like long-necks!"

"But the women think they look beautiful," said Tio. "It's part of their tradition. For me, I think it is part of their bondage."

"How much does it weigh?" asked a teenager. "How can they hold their heads up?"

Tio lifted his palms upward. "They're used to it. I think the coils weigh maybe thirty or forty pounds."

Alonzo and the children gazed as the women came closer and closer. What odd-looking women! Besides their long necks with coiled neck bands, they wore pounds and pounds of beads and charms, hanging down from their necks and around their wrists. Their hair was bound up like a pyramid, full of combs and pins.

As the Lennite women approached, they saw the Karen children and were puzzled. But when they saw Alonzo, they gasped in astonishment. They had never seen a pale foreigner. And one with red hair! They nearly lost their footing and turned as if they would run back down the mountain.

"Don't be afraid!" called Tio in their language. "We come in peace. We come with special news for your village."

The women began to chatter to each other in a language that Alonzo didn't understand. Tio told him they had decided that since so many children had come with the two men, the Karen man must be harmless.

The women shouldered their loads once again and hurried as fast as they could up the cliff to the village, in order to try to be the first to announce the astonishing news.

"Teacher, let's go!" cried one of the children. He pulled on Alonzo's hand, and off they started again, climbing bit by bit up the steep path, hanging on to roots and jutting rocks.

What a sight greeted them at the village of Lennite. Alonzo took a minute just to let the sight sink in. Rocks and boulders everywhere, with crude bamboo huts squeezed here and there between them. Hoards of half-wild dogs, barking and howling. Dozens of pigs, squealing and running from place to place. Crowds of people running and, and when they saw Alonzo, pointing and calling to each other. Fear radiated from their large eyes.

In the midst of the hullaballoo, Alonzo, Tio, and the young people set up the big tent on some rocks where there was no hut. Behind them, yet another cliff towered high above, into the sky. One of the young people got out the accordion and began to play. The children and young people gathered in neat rows to sing. They sang in the Karen language, so the Padaungs couldn't understand them. But the sound of the music made them stop and stare.

"Rock of ages, cleft for me, let me hide myself in Thee."

Mr. Bunker, sitting on a rock beside the children, looked out over the crowd of people in the village. More and more were gathering—there must be several hundred of them, fearful, curious, staring, open-mouthed, pointing. Becoming quieter and quieter.

"Let the water and the blood, from Thy wounded side which flowed
Be of sin the double cure, save from wrath, and make me sure."

As the children sang, Alonzo observed. All around the village he saw skulls skewered on bamboo poles, skulls of dogs, pigs, and other animals that he couldn't even identify. *Living in fear, even in this remote place,* he thought. *No matter how remote they become, they still can't get away from the nats. They can't escape fear.* Altars of bamboo, for pouring out drink offerings to the spirits, stood here and there. The terrible smell that wafted through the village came not only from the unwashed bodies but also from the rotten eggs and molding food placed all around in bamboo baskets—more efforts to keep the spirits away. A dog nosed at the rotten food, but a little child kicked the dog away before running to take his place at the front of the crowd seating themselves in a semi-circle around the children.

"Not the labors of my hands could fulfill the law's demands.
Could my zeal no languor know, could my tears forever flow,
These for sin could not atone. Thou must save, and thou alone!"

The strange, haunting music floated over the heads of the Padaung people of Lennite. The men and women of the village stood behind the village children silent, dark staring eyes empty, angry, fearful, hopeless.

"O Lord Jesus my Savior," Alonzo prayed silently as the notes of the song floated on the air. "This is the great test of Your powerful Gospel. Can You—no, *will* You—lift these benighted souls out of heathen demon appeasement to the freedom and beauty and glory that You offer in Your resurrection life?"

When the song had ended, the missionary Tio stood up to preach in the language of the Padaungs.

"O people of Lennite!" he proclaimed. "I come to bring you good news of hope from the great Yuwah!"

The great Yuwah? Once again, as had been happening for decades now, a new tribe was hearing for the first time that the great Yuwah had returned to them with a gift of hope. The effect was electric. All eyes focused on Tio.

"The great Yuwah is full of goodness, full of light. He has no badness, no darkness." As Tio spoke, the Padaungs raised their eyebrows in agreement and stared.

"You people," Tio continued. "You are full of badness and darkness."

Alonzo listened and watched, wondering how the Padaungs would respond. But they raised their eyebrows again.

"You have heard through the generations that forgiveness for your sins is impossible. For this, you think that you must sacrifice to the nats."

The people listened and watched.

"But I have brought the white Book that has been lost from our people for so long!" Tio held up his open

Bible, and the people stared at the white pages. "This Book tells us that the great Yuwah has made a way of forgiveness, because of His great love. His own Son has come to earth to take the payment for your sins. You can again live in the light of Yuwah."

Tio finished speaking and sat down. Immediately the men of Lennite began to argue with each other.

"This is a voice from the heavens!" cried one. "We are hearing from Yuwah Himself! We must welcome Him to come and live among us!"

But another said, "If Yuwah comes to live among us, then we can no longer attack other villages. The other villages will no longer be afraid of us, and they'll come and destroy us."

"But we could have peace with our neighbors," said another.

"Yes," replied Tio. "If you came to Yuwah through Jesu Cree, you can live in peace."

"But if we bow down before Yuwah, we can no longer make our whiskey and get drunk with it," another protested.

Another asked, "Would we have to treat our women equally? Then we would never control them."

"Yes, you will honor your women and treat them as your equals," said Tio. "This is a better way."

"Huh," snorted the men. They wanted nothing to do with such an ignorant way of life.

"But if we came to Yuwah, we might sometimes have enough to eat." An old man lifted his quavering voice.

The rest of the day the men of Lennite argued, and on into the night, as Tio spoke truths of the Christian life from the white Book. The women and children crept away, quiet, fearful, not fully understanding what was happening.

Alonzo settled in the tent with the young people for the night, but little sleep came to him. He spent the night praying for Tio and the people of Lennite, as the great battle raged in the village, the battle of the spirits against the Spirit.

Early in the morning, one of the older Karen boys shook Alonzo Bunker from his fitful sleep. "Teacher!" he cried. "We won! They want to worship Yuwah!"

"All of them?" Alonzo asked in surprise. He had prayed all night and had fallen asleep only toward morning.

"Yes, all of them! They've already killed a pig and eaten it to seal their agreement!"

By the time he came out of the tent, Alonzo saw a big bonfire beginning to blaze, and people throwing things on it. Old animal skulls, baskets of rotten eggs and meat, bamboo altars, all were being destroyed and thrown on the fire.

Though some of the villagers were silent, many of them cried out in joy.

"God has done a great work here," Tio observed to Alonzo.

Alonzo gazed at the sight. "We can't leave them," he said. "They have no Scriptures in their language. Will you stay and teach them?"

Tio rubbed his face with his hands. "I thought you might ask me that," he said. "You know I'm already pastoring two churches back in our home on the other side of the mountains."

"Yes," Alonzo agreed. "And I know you have a beautiful little house and a garden. But we'll be here a few more days. Will you spend that time praying about what God wants you to do?"

As they spoke, one of the young men from Lennite approached and spoke rapidly. "Teacher," he said, addressing Tio. "Will you stay and teach us about Yuwah and his way?"

Tio smiled. "I'll ask Yuwah what He wants. But I think I know the answer."

See Thinking Further for Chapter 16 on page 142.

17. THE WILDERNESS BLOSSOMED LIKE A ROSE

To stayed at the Lennite village. Though the people gladly built him a hut to be a house, a chapel, and a school all in one, he found that many of them really hadn't desired to follow Yuwah. Many of them turned back to their old ways.

After two more years of work in this hard place, in 1891, Tio finally baptized the first Christians of Lennite village. Bit by bit real change began to take place. Some of the younger women decided to take off their neck rings, even in the face of their parents' anger.

After four more years, sixty people had joined the church, and Tio was happy with their true faith. "Let's invite the Annual Conference to meet at our new village!" the Christians said. That meant that over seven hundred people would be coming. The non-Christians, who now lived in peace, didn't object.

Messengers were sent out, and the pastors agreed. For the first time in seven years Alonzo Bunker trekked out to visit the village of Lennite. Once again Pastor Tio acted as his guide.

"But where is the village now?" Alonzo asked as he gazed toward the top of the steep cliff. "I'm glad I don't have to climb up there!"

"No," Tio chuckled. "They no longer live in fear, just as we told them. Come and see the new village."

They hiked around the base of the cliff and came in sight of the new community. A wonder met their eyes.

"This is what God has done!" Tio said proudly, extending his arm.

Alonzo gazed around at the new village. It was situated on a sloping mountainside, right next to a sparkling mountain stream, so that the women had to do almost no work to fetch the water. It was clean and orderly, with neat little bamboo houses standing here and there. The ground was swept clean, and tables and benches adorned the village area. The people who approached the mission party looked clean and fresh, happy and unafraid.

"You see the chapel?" Tio pointed to a wooden building large enough for the Annual Conference. "We built that with our own hands! And thirteen more people have come forward for baptism into the Christ-life!"

"Welcome, welcome!" sang the people of the village. "We're ready for you! We have slaughtered pigs for you!

Yuwah has given us peace in our hearts, and we praise Him!" As more and more missionaries and other Karen Christians came, they were led to neat bamboo huts that had been built just for them.

"The people here have been preparing for the Annual Conference for a year," Tio said. "Some of them even traveled for two days to bring back that rose bush." He pointed to a blooming bush, gloriously covered with sweet-smelling roses. "I remember Isaiah," he added. " 'The wilderness shall rejoice and blossom like a rose.' This is that wilderness."

At the meeting, one Christian stood up to speak. "We have learned what true worship is," he said. "We never worshipped the nats, we only feared them. We offered sacrifices to them in order to make them leave us alone. That was nat appeasement."

The visiting Christians nodded in agreement.

"But now," the man stretched out his arms in joy, "We know true worship. Yuwah is the one who alone is deserving of true worship! True worship is given in love and thanksgiving and praise, because our hearts overflow!"

For three days the Christians of Lennite welcomed their seven hundred visitors and praised God with them and prayed with them, their hearts overflowing with joy.

Alonzo Bunker stood and watched, holding a Karen Bible with its white, white pages. He remembered the sin and darkness and fear he had seen when he first visited. "Truly, O God, truly, O Yuwah," he prayed, "You have done a great work." His eyes turned to the huge bouquet of roses on one of the tables. "You have made this wilderness blossom like a rose."

See Thinking Further for Chapter 17 on page 143.

A MESSAGE FROM THE AUTHOR

In 1981 Don Richardson (who was a missionary featured in Hidden Heroes #3, *Witness Men*) wrote a book called *Eternity in Their Hearts*. This book described how, when the gospel of Jesus Christ had come to people groups all over the world, many of these peoples embraced the truth because their hearts had been prepared through old legends or old memories or old prophecies. The Karen nation was one, and the story of the Guardian of the Book especially made an impression on me. I thought, "I want to write these stories for children to read."

That was thirty years ago. God, in His wisdom, had other plans for me for many years, including raising four children; homeschooling for twenty-five years; being involved in church and homeschool groups; writing three Christian biographies; and growing deeper, through His Word, in the delight over who Jesus Christ is in and for and through me.

When I began to write the Hidden Heroes series, I hadn't forgotten about the Karen tribes. In 2012 when I undertook the research for this book, I discovered two things. One, to my delight, all the books about the Karen tribes written in the 1800s and early 1900s, and many of the journals and missionary bulletins, were now available online for easy access, any time of day or night.

But second, and more important, I found that no one had ever written this story of the conversion of the Karen tribes for children—the story that began with Adoniram Judson and continued for over a hundred years. I felt astounded and privileged. I still do, even as I write this message to you. God is doing great things around the world, and I get to be a part of it through these books. A dream of my youth has come to pass.

ABOUT THE MISSIONARIES OR HOW MUCH OF THIS STORY IS REALLY TRUE?

That's a good question. And I want to answer it as carefully as I can.

The story of the Karen people is real. Their legends are real. Every name of every missionary and every Karen person is a real name of a real person who really lived and really did the things that are described in this book. Everything that everyone says in this book is either taken directly from people's diaries and newsletters and books, or else reconstructed as accurately as possible according to research of the time and the people.

Chapter 1 – Keeper of the Stories
This legend is told almost word for word as a Karen man related it years later to a "pale foreigner," one of the American missionaries, in the book *Soo Thah: A Tale of the Making of the Karen Nation* by Alonzo Bunker, published in 1902. Thabew, who entered Adoniram Judson's life as an older man, would surely have heard this legend around the fire.

(*Name and spelling*: Burma is now usually called "Myanmar," though not all people of this country agree as to what their country's name should be. In most of the older sources, *Yuwah* is spelled *Yuah*. Thabew's name is spelled a number of different ways in the old books, most commonly Tha Byu or Thah Pyu or some combination of those words. Usually his name has the title "Ko" in front of it, a term of respect like "Mr." that literally means "older brother.")

Chapter 2 — Waiting for the Pale Brother
Adoniram Judson, the leader of the first significant missionary group to Burma, is also considered the Father of the Modern Missionary Movement in the United States.

George Boardman was a missionary to Burma from 1825 to 1831, when he died at the age of thirty. No biography has been written about him (that I could find), perhaps because he died so young. His journal, published in 1834, provided most of the information for this chapter.

Thabew's story is told more fully in *The Karen Apostle* by Francis Mason, published in 1843.

Many of the details about the Karen people and their customs come from the book *The Karen People of Burma: A Study in Anthropology and Ethnology* by Harry Ignatius Marshall, published in 1922.

(*Name and spelling* Tavoy is now called "Dawei." Maulmein, which was also spelled Moulmein, is now spelled Mawlmein or Mawlamyine.)

Chapters 3-5 — Why Have You Come? and *Is it the Lost Book of Yuwah?* and *More! More!*

The quotation from the "little book," is actually from a booklet that Adoniram Judson wrote in Burmese, *A Creed, in Twelve Articles; or, A Summary of the Doctrine of the Lord Jesus Christ. By Adoniram Judson, for the People of Burma,* which can be found with an internet search. The corresponding Karen legend is given, word for translated word, from the traditions of the people.

Besides *The Memoirs of George Boardman*, these stories are told in several other books. The most helpful to me was *The Gospel in Burma* by Mrs. Macleod Wylie, published in 1860. (Ladies used their husbands' names more in those days.)

(*Name note*: Siam is now called Thailand.)

Chapter 9 —Farewell to Teacher Boardman

Almost everything in these chapters came directly from the Boardmans' journals or letters, especially the letters of George Boardman's wife, Sarah.

Sarah Boardman became a widow at the age of thirty. But she dedicated herself to God even as a widow, and determined to continue the work of teaching among the Burmans. Adoniram Judson, who had lost his wife, Ann, about three years earlier, eventually asked Sarah to marry him. She worked with him in Burma until shortly before her death.

Chapters 11- 13 — Missionary to the Wild Men; Wild Men Clear the Way; and The End of the Reign of the Nats

Alonzo Bunker, though he wrote two books that were very helpful to me, was such a hidden hero that I was unable to discover exactly what years he worked with the Hill Tribes of Burma, though I believe that it was approximately 1860 to 1905.

Su Yah is the real name of the national missionary that Alonzo Bunker calls Soo Thah in his book *Soo Thah, a Tale of the Making of the Karen Nation*, published in 1902. (I never did understand why he decided to change the name when he wrote the book!)

(*Name notes:* I changed the spelling of the first part of the Karen missionary's name from *Soo* to *Su*, because that fits the pattern of spelling changes that have taken place in the last hundred years. For example, the spelling "Hindoo" has changed to *Hindu*, and "Boodhist" has changed to *Buddhist*. The Christian Brec village, which I called Letcho, really has a much longer name, "Saupalecho.")

Chapters 14-17 — A Battle of the Spirits and *Singing the Battle; The Village of Long-Necks* and *The Wilderness Blossomed Like a Rose*

The Karen people were—and are—known to be great singers with beautiful voices. Many times through my research I saw missionaries commenting on what beautiful voices they had, able to quickly pick up both melody and harmony. All three of these stories of singing are found in *Sketches from the Karen Hills* by Alonzo Bunker, published in 1910.

The American Baptist Missionary Magazine, which began publication in the early 1800s with Adoniram Judson's work in Burma, now has many of its annual volumes available online, full of letters and journals and reports from the missionaries themselves, much of which made fascinating reading. I could see that there were enough stories about the Karen tribes for a much larger book, or a second volume, but perhaps I'll leave that adventure for someone else to pursue. I hope someone will.

THINKING FURTHER

Chapter 1- Keeper of the Stories

Romans 5:12, 14: *Therefore, just as sin came into the world through one man, and death through sin, and so death spread to all men because all sinned … Yet death reigned from Adam to Moses, even over those whose sinning was not like the transgression of Adam, who was a type of the one who was to come.*

Name some parts of the old man's stories that were the same as the Creation Story in Genesis. Name some things that were different. Why do you think some parts were different?

Chapter 2 - Waiting for the Pale Brother

Matthew 4:10 : *Then Jesus said to him, "Be gone, Satan! For it is written, 'You shall worship the Lord your God, and him only shall you serve.' "*

Why were the men doing the strange things they did? How did the women's song sound hopeful? Why do you think they didn't understand it? What did it mean?

"Appeasement" is offering sacrifices out of fear, not love. "Worship" is honor born of love and thanksgiving. Why did Thabew tell George Boardman that his people didn't worship anyone?

Chapter 3 - A Fire Inside Me

2 Timothy 1:6-7 *For this reason I remind you to fan into flame the gift of God, which is in you through the laying on of my*

hands, for God gave us a spirit not of fear but of power and love and self-control.

How did Thabew seem very different from the Burmans to George Boardman?

The Karens were known as a very meek and fearful people. How was Thabew different?

Why did Adoniram Judson say Thabew couldn't be baptized yet? How did George Boardman indicate that this problem could be turned to something good?

Chapter 4 - Why Have You Come?

Romans 10:14: *How then will they call on him in whom they have not believed? And how are they to believe in him of whom they have never heard? And how are they to hear without someone preaching?*

Why did the men want to travel for three days to meet George Boardman? Were the men worshiping the book? Why? George Boardman thought they were atheists. Was he right? Why did he think this?

Chapter 5 - Is it the Lost Book of Yuwah?

Psalm 90:1-2: *Lord, you have been our dwelling place in all generations. Before the mountains were brought forth, or ever you had formed the earth and the world, from everlasting to everlasting you are God.*

Why did the Karen man tell George Boardman that their beliefs were the same as his? Tell some specific ways they were the same.

Why were the Karen men so surprised to hear George call Thabew "brother"? What special meaning did that expression have to them?

Chapter 6 - More! More!

Isaiah 52:7: *How beautiful upon the mountains are the feet of him who brings good news, who publishes peace, who brings good news of happiness, who publishes salvation, who says to Zion, "Your God reigns."*

Why were the people so eager to hear the words of Thabew? One of them had become a Buddhist. What was he looking for in the Buddhist religion? How did he know he could find it in the words Thabew was preaching?

Apostle means "official messenger." Why was Thabew called the Karen Apostle?

Chapter 7 - The Guardian of the Book

Luke 4:8: *And Jesus answered him, "It is written, 'You shall worship the Lord your God, and him only shall you serve.' "*

What did the song mean that the people sang when they worshiped the book? Do you think they understood the meaning?

Why was it wrong to worship the book? What should they have done with it instead?

Chapter 8 - Funeral Battle in Chikku

I Corinthians 15:16-17; 42-45: *For if the dead are not raised, not even Christ has been raised. And if Christ has not been raised, your faith is futile and you are still in your sins. ... So is it with the resurrection of the dead. What is sown is perishable; what is raised is imperishable. It is sown in dishonor; it is raised in glory. It is sown in weakness; it is raised in power. It is sown a natural body; it is raised a spiritual body. If there is a natural body, there is also a spiritual body. Thus it is written, "The first man Adam became a living being"; the last Adam became a life-giving spirit.*

Why does this chapter talk about a "battle"—what kind of battle was it?

Why did the non-Christian people of the tribe feel so hopeless? What are some ways they expressed their hopelessness? What are some ways the new Christians expressed their hope?

Chapter 9 - Sleepless Delight in Chikku

Matthew 11:28: *Come to me, all who labor and are heavy laden, and I will give you rest.*

Long ago one of the Karen songs had promised that when the great worship came, they would be unable to sleep. How was that promise fulfilled when the pale brother came?

Why was George Boardman struggling in his heart? What promise did the Lord give him?

George Boardman preached from three different Scriptures. Tell how each one was important for the Karen people.

Chapter 10 - Farewell to Teacher Boardman

Philippians 1:20: *... it is my eager expectation and hope that I will not be at all ashamed, but that with full courage now as always Christ will be honored in my body, whether by life or by death.*

The Karens might have thought that when "happiness" came, it would mean they would have a comfortable life. How did George Boardman's life show them something different? Why do you suppose it made such a deep impression on them?

George Boardman died when he was only thirty. If he had stayed in America, he might have been able to live another forty or fifty years. How do you know he and Sarah didn't make a foolish decision?

Chapter 11 - Missionary to the Wild Men

Romans 10:14: *How then will they call on him in whom they have not believed? And how are they to believe in him of whom they have never heard? And how are they to hear without someone preaching?*

Describe how the gospel had spread among the Karens in the fifty years since Thabew began preaching. How had they changed? Was this change good or bad?

Why was Su Yah unafraid? Do you think he should have been afraid? What did he know about the Brec people? What did Su Yah see in the Brec village when he arrived? Why did the wild men drop their weapons?

Chapter 12 - Wild Men Clear the Way

Isaiah 40:3-5: *A voice cries: "In the wilderness prepare the way of the LORD; make straight in the desert a highway for our God. Every valley shall be lifted up, and every mountain and hill be made low; the uneven ground shall become level, and the rough places a plain. And the glory of the LORD shall be revealed, and all flesh shall see it together, for the mouth of the LORD has spoken."*

Why did the wild men come to the Annual Assembly? How did they react? What did they do to show that they wanted someone to come and teach them more?

Chapter 13 - The End of the Reign of the Nats

Isaiah 61:1: *The Spirit of the Lord God is upon me, because the LORD has anointed me to bring good news to the poor; he has sent me to bind up the brokenhearted, to proclaim liberty to the captives, and the opening of the prison to those who are bound.*

What did Su Yah preach that the Brecs knew was true? How was this similar to being released from prison?

In this story, the missionaries destroyed all the spirit items. In later years, missionaries in various places around the world realized it would be better to insist that the new Christians should destroy all their old spirit items themselves. Why do you think they made that decision?

Chapter 14 - A Battle of the Spirits

Exodus 9:7b: *But the heart of Pharaoh was hardened, and he did not let the people go.*

Why did the people of Letcho think that this was a battle of the spirits instead of a battle of people? Why did they think it was wrong to take up weapons against them?

The men of Letcho compared their battle to three different battles of the Old Testament. How was their battle similar to each one?

Chapter 15 - Singing the Battle

2 Chronicles 20:21-22: *And when he had taken counsel with the people, he appointed those who were to sing to the LORD and praise him in holy attire, as they went before the army, and say, "Give thanks to the LORD, for his steadfast love endures forever." And when they began to sing and praise, the LORD set an ambush against the men of Ammon, Moab, and Mount Seir, who had come against Judah, so that they were routed.*

The people of Letcho fought their battle with prayer and singing. Read the full story of Jehoshaphat in 2 Chronicles 20 and compare the two stories.

Chapter 16 - The Village of Long-Necks

Ephesians 6:12: *For we do not wrestle against flesh and blood, but against the rulers, against the authorities, against the cosmic powers over this present darkness, against the spiritual forces of evil in the heavenly places.*

Why did the Lennites live in such a remote location?

What were some reasons some of the Lennites didn't want to come to Jesus Christ? Why did they think those were good reasons?

What was one reason some Lennites did want to come to Christ? These are called "felt needs." Sometimes felt needs can lead people to their real needs of salvation and peace with God.

A lot of arguing took place over the next few hours. Where was the real battle taking place?

Chapter 17 - The Wilderness Blossomed like a Rose
Isaiah 35:1 (KJV): *The wilderness and the solitary place shall be glad for them; and the desert shall rejoice, and blossom as the rose.*

The people of the Lennite village changed in many ways in the seven years since Alonzo Bunker had first visited. Name some of the ways they changed.

People's beliefs affects what they value. What they value affects what they do. Name some ways the beliefs and values of the people of Lennite had changed in order for their actions to change so much.

CHRISTIAN FOCUS PUBLICATIONS

Christian Focus | Christian Heritage | CF4K | Mentor

Christian Focus Publications publishes books for adults and children under its four main imprints: Christian Focus, CF4K, Mentor and Christian Heritage. Our books reflect our conviction that God's Word is reliable and Jesus is the way to know him, and live for ever with him.

Our children's publication list covers pre-school to early teens. We also publish personal and family devotional titles, biographies and inspirational stories that children will love.

From pre-school board books to teenage apologetics, we have it covered!

Christian Focus Publications Ltd,
Geanies House, Fearn, Ross-shire,
IV20 1TW, Scotland,
United Kingdom.
www.christianfocus.com

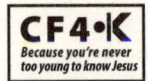

CF4•K
Because you're never
too young to know Jesus